LITTLE BOOK OF

# Kings & Queens

## OF ENGLAND

Martine Pugh

LITTLE BOOK OF

# Kings &
# Queens
## OF ENGLAND

First published in the UK in 2014

© Demand Media Limited 2014

www.demand-media.co.uk

Printed and bound in Europe

ISBN 978-1-910270-03-5

# Contents

# King Egbert

Egbert, King of Wessex (802-39), and the first Saxon king recognized as sovereign of all England. He was the son of a Kentish noble but claimed descent from Cerdic founder of Wessex. During the late 8th century, when King Offa of Mercia ruled most of England, Egbert lived in exile at the court of Charlemagne.

In 802 Egbert returned from exile and became King of Wessex. He conquered the kingdoms of Kent, Cornwall, and Mercia (now known as the Midlands), and by 830 he was also acknowledged as sovereign of East Anglia, Sussex, Surrey, and Northumbria and was given the title of Bretwalda ("ruler of the British").

During following years Egbert led expeditions against the Welsh and the Vikings. The year before his death he defeated a combined force of Cornish and Viking armies at Hingston Down in Cornwall.

| | |
|---|---|
| Name: | King Egbert |
| Born: | c.769 |
| Parents: | Ealhmund of Kent (Father) |
| House of: | Wessex |
| Became King: | 802 |
| Married: | Redburh of Francia |
| Children: | 1 son |
| Died: | 839 |
| Buried at: | Winchester |
| Succeeded by: | His son Ethelwulf (Æthelwulf) |

# King Ethelwulf
## (Æhelwulf)

Ethelwulf, meaning "Noble Wolf" was the only known child of King Egbert of Wessex. He conquered the kingdom of Kent on behalf of his father in 825, and was later made King of Kent as a sub-king to his father. When Egbert died Ethelwulf succeeded as King of Wessex. At the same time his eldest son Ethelstan became sub-king of Kent as a subordinate ruler.

His reign is characterized by Viking invasions common to all English rulers of the time, but the making of war was not his chief claim to fame. Ethelwulf is remembered as a highly religious man who cared about the establishment and preservation of the church. He was also wealthy and controlled vast resources.

In 855, about a year after the death of his first wife he accompanied his son, Alfred, on a pilgrimage to Rome. He distributed gold to the clergy of St. Peter's and offered them chalices of the purest gold and silver-gilt candelabra of Saxon work. During the return

| | |
|---|---|
| Born: | 795 at Aachen |
| Parents: | Egbert and Redburh |
| House of: | Wessex |
| Became King: | 839 |
| Married: | (1) Osburh (2) Judith of Flanders |
| Children: | 6 |
| Died: | January 13, 858 |
| Buried at: | Winchester |
| Succeeded by: | His son Ethelbald (Æthelbald) |

journey in 856 he married his second wife, Judith of Flanders, a Frankish princess and a great-granddaughter of Charlemagne. She was about 12 years old, the daughter of Charles the Bald, King of the West Franks.

# King Ethelbald
## (Æhelbald)

While his father, Ethelwulf, was on pilgrimage to Rome in 855, Ethelbald plotted with the Bishop of Sherbourne and the ealdorman of Somerset against him. The details of the plot are unknown, but upon his return from Rome, Ethelwulf found his direct authority limited to the sub-kingdom of Kent, while Ethelbald controlled Wessex.

When his father died in 858, full control passed to Ethelbald who married his father's widow Judith. However under pressure from the church the marriage was annulled after a year. Perhaps Ethelbald's premature power grab was prompted by impatience, or greed, or lack of confidence in his father's succession plans.

Whatever the case, he did not live long to enjoy it. He died in 860, passing the throne to his brother, Ethelbert.

| | |
|---|---|
| Born: | c.831 |
| Parents: | Æthelwulf and Osburh |
| House of: | Wessex |
| Became King: | 858 |
| Married: | Judith (his step mother) |
| Children: | None |
| Died: | December 20, 860 |
| Buried at: | Sherbourne Abbey |
| Succeeded by: | His brother Ethelbert |

# King Ethelbert
## (Æhelberht)

RIGHT Statue of Ethelbert, Lady Wootton's Green Canterbury

FAR RIGHT Depiction of Ethelbert , 13th-century manuscript in the British Library

During his reign the Danes returned and soon after his accession a Danish army landed either via the Thames or on the south coast and advanced as far as Winchester before two contingents of Saxons defeated them. Like his father and brother he was also crowned at Kingston upon Thames.

The Anglo-Saxon Chronicle describes Ethelbert's reign as one of good harmony and lasting peace. Though this was true of internal affairs, the Vikings remained a great threat, unsuccessfully storming Winchester and ravaging eastern Kent.

One development was that Wessex and its recent south-eastern conquests became a united kingdom.

Unlike his predecessors, Ethelbert did not appoint another member of his family as under-king of Kent.

| | |
|---|---|
| Born: | c.834 |
| Parents: | Aethelwulf and Osburh |
| House of: | Wessex |
| Became King: | 860 |
| Married: | Unmarried |
| Children: | 2 sons |
| Died: | 866 |
| Buried at: | Sherbourne |
| Succeeded by: | His brother Ethelred |

# King Ethelred I
## (The Pious)

Ethelred succeeded his brother Ethelbert. Ethelred spent all his time ruling from the battlefield, and his reign was one long struggle against the Danes. Ivarr the Boneless and his brother Halfdan based in Dublin attacked and occupied York in 866 which became a Viking kingdom (Jorvik). The Danes marched south and occupied Nottingham.

In 869 they sailed to East Anglia where they killed the local king Edmund. Wessex was then threatened and Ethelred and his brother Alfred were engaged in a series of battles with the Danes Ivarr, Halfdan and Guthrun at Reading, Ashdown and Basing. During 870/871 the Danes sacked and plundered their way through the countryside. The next major engagement was at Meretun, in Hampshire, which was an indecisive battle. Ethelred was seriously injured in the battle and died of his wounds at Witchampton, near Wimbourne, where he was buried.

His two sons were considered too young to be king, so his brother Alfred succeeded to the throne instead.

| | |
|---|---|
| Born: | c.837 |
| Parents: | Æthelwulf and Osburh |
| House of: | Wessex |
| Became King: | 866 |
| Married: | Wulfrida |
| Children: | 2 sons |
| Died: | April 23, 871 |
| Buried at: | Wimbourne |
| Succeeded by: | His brother Alfred |

# King Alfred
## "The Great"

Anglo-Saxon king 871–899 who defended England against Danish invasion and founded the first English navy. He succeeded his brother Ethelred to the throne of Wessex in 871, and a new legal code came into force during his reign. He encouraged the translation of scholarly works from Latin (some he translated himself), and promoted the development of the Anglo-Saxon Chronicle. This ensured that his deeds were recorded in history as legends and we know more about him than any other Anglo Saxon King.

| | |
|---|---|
| Born: | c.849 at Wantage, Berkshire |
| Parents: | Æthelwulf and Osburh |
| House of: | Wessex |
| Became King: | 871 |
| Married: | Ealhswith of Mercia |
| Children: | 5 |
| Died | October 26, 899 |
| Buried at: | Winchester |
| Succeeded by: | His son Edward |

Alfred was born at Wantage, the youngest son of Ethelwulf (d. 858). In 870 Alfred and his brother Ethelred fought many battles against the Danes. Alfred defeated the Danes at Ashdown in 871, and succeeded Ethelred as king in April 871. Not all his campaigns were so successful; on a number of occasions he had to resort to buying off the Danes for a brief respite. Five years of uneasy peace followed while the Danes were occupied in other parts of England. In 876 the Danes attacked again, and in 878 Alfred was forced to retire to the Somerset marshes. The legend of him burning the cakes probably comes from this period.

In 878, he again defeated the Danes in the Battle of Edington. They made peace and Guthrum, their king, was baptised with Alfred as his sponsor. In 886 AD, Alfred negotiated a treaty with the Danes. England was divided, with the north and the east (between the Rivers Thames and Tees) declared to be Danish territory – later known as the 'Danelaw'. Alfred therefore secured the survival of Wessex. The Anglo-Saxon Chronicle says that following his capture of London in 886 'all the English people submitted to him, except those who were in captivity to the Danes'. In some respects, therefore, Alfred could be considered the first king of England. A new landing in Kent encouraged a revolt of the East Anglian Danes, which was suppressed 884–86, and after the final foreign invasion was defeated 892–96, Alfred built up the defences of his kingdom to ensure that it was not threatened by the Danes again. He organized his army and built a series of well-defended settlements across

ABOVE Portrait of King Alfred the Great

southern England. He also established a navy for use against the Danish raiders who continued to harass the coast.

Alfred established a code of laws and a reformed coinage. He had a strong belief in the importance of education and learnt Latin in his late thirties. He then arranged, and took part in, the translation of books from Latin to Anglo-Saxon.

Alfred died in October 899 AD and was buried at his capital city of Winchester.

# King Edward
## "The Elder"

King of the West Saxons. He succeeded his father Alfred the Great in 899. When Alfred died, Edward's cousin Æthelwold, the son of King Ethelred, rose up to claim the throne and so began Æthelwold's Revolt. He seized Wimborne and Christchurch. Edward marched to Badbury and offered battle, but Æthelwold refused to leave Wimborne. Just when it looked as if Edward was going to attack Wimborne, Æthelwold left in the night, and joined the Danes in Northumbria, where he was announced as King. In the meantime, Edward was crowned on 8 June 900.

In 901, Æthelwold came with a fleet to Essex, and encouraged the Danes in East Anglia to rise up. In the following year he attacked English Mercia and northern Wessex. Edward retaliated by ravaging East Anglia, but when he retreated south the men of Kent disobeyed the order to retire, and were intercepted by the Danish army. The two sides met at the Battle of the Holme on 13 December 902. According to the Anglo-Saxon Chronicle, the Danes "kept the place of slaughter", but they suffered heavy losses, including Æthelwold.

| | |
|---|---|
| Born: | c.871 |
| Parents: | Alfred the Great and Ealswith of Mercia |
| House of: | Wessex |
| Became King: | 899 |
| Married: | (1) Ecgywn (2) Elfleda & (3) Edgiva. |
| Children: | 5 sons and 11 daughters |
| Died: | July 17, 924 |
| Buried at: | Winchester |
| Succeeded by: | His son Æthelstan |

In 909, Edward sent an army to harass Northumbria. In the following year, the Northumbrians retaliated by attacking Mercia, but they were met by the combined Mercian and West Saxon army at the Battle of Tettenhall, where the Northumbrian Danes were destroyed. From that point, they never raided south of the River Humber. Edward then began the construction of a number of fortresses (burhs), to kept the Danes at bay.

Edward extended the control of Wessex over the whole of Mercia, East Anglia and Essex, conquering lands occupied by the Danes and bringing the residual autonomy of Mercia to an end in 918, after the death of his sister, Æthelflæd. Æthelflæd's daughter, Ælfwynn, was named as her successor, but Edward deposed her, bringing Mercia under his direct control. He had already annexed the cities of London and Oxford and the surrounding lands of Oxfordshire and Middlesex in 911. The first half of the tenth century was critical in the development of the shire as principal administrative unit in England, and Edward was probably responsible for shiring Mercia and the eastern Danelaw. By 918, all of the Danes south of the Humber had submitted to him. By the end of his reign, the Norse, the Scots and the Welsh had acknowledged him as "father and lord".

He died leading an army against a Welsh-Mercian rebellion, on 17 July 924 at Farndon-Upon-Dee and was buried in the New Minster in Winchester, Hampshire, which he himself had established in 901. Edward's body was transferred to Hyde Abbey. His last resting place is currently marked by a cross-inscribed stone slab within the outline of the old abbey marked out in a public park.

ABOVE Depiction of King Edward

# King Athelstan

Athelstan was the first king of all England, and Alfred the Great's grandson. He reigned between 925 and 939 AD. A distinguished and courageous soldier, he pushed the boundaries of the kingdom to the furthest extent they had yet reached.

In 927 AD he took York from the Danes, and forced the submission of

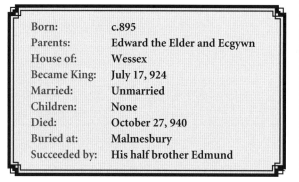

| | |
|---|---|
| Born: | c.895 |
| Parents: | Edward the Elder and Ecgywn |
| House of: | Wessex |
| Became King: | July 17, 924 |
| Married: | Unmarried |
| Children: | None |
| Died: | October 27, 940 |
| Buried at: | Malmesbury |
| Succeeded by: | His half brother Edmund |

Constantine, King of Scotland and of the northern kings. All five of the Welsh kings agreed to pay a huge annual tribute. He also eliminated opposition in Cornwall. In 937 AD, at the Battle of Brunanburh, Athelstan led a force drawn from Britain, and defeated an invasion made by the king of Scotland, in alliance with the Welsh and Danes, from Dublin.

Under Athelstan, law codes strengthened royal control over his large kingdom; currency was regulated to control silver's weight and to penalise fraudsters; buy-ing and selling was largely confined to the burhs, encouraging town life; and areas of settlement in the Midlands and Danish towns were consolidated into shires. Overseas, Athelstan built alliances by marrying off four of his half sisters to various rulers in western Europe.

He was also a great collector of works of art and religious relics, which he gave away to many of his followers and churches in order to gain their support. He died in 939 AD, and was buried in Malmesbury Abbey.

BELOW The tomb of King Athelstan in Malmesbury Abbey

# King Edmund

RIGHT Depiction of King Edmund , 14th-century manuscript

King of England 939–46. The son of Edward the Elder, he succeeded his half-brother, Athelstan, as king in 939. He succeeded in regaining control of Mercia, which on his accession had fallen to the Norse inhabitants of Northumbria, and of the Five Boroughs, an independent confederation within the Danelaw.

In 945 Edmund ravaged Strathclyde and killed its troublesome King, Donald MacDonald. He returned the Kingdom to its Scottish overlord, Malcolm I, thus recognising Northumbria as the northern limit of Anglo-Saxon England.

As well as uniting England, he bolstered his authority by allowing St Dunstan to reform the Benedictine order.

On 26 May 946, Edmund was murdered by Leofa, an exiled thief, while attending St Augustine's Day mass in Pucklechurch (South Gloucestershire)

| | |
|---|---|
| Born: | c.922 |
| Parents: | Edward the Elder and Edgiva |
| House of: | Wessex |
| Became King: | October 27, 940 |
| Married: | 1) Elgiva (2) Ethelfleda |
| Children: | 2 sons |
| Died: | May 26, 946 |
| Buried at: | Glastonbury |
| Succeeded by: | His brother Edred |

# King Edred

King Edred was born in about 923 AD, a son of King Edward the Elder by his third marriage. He succeeded his brother, King Edmund I, in 946. The same year, on 16 August, Edred was consecrated by Archbishop Oda of Canterbury at Kingston upon Thames (Surrey, now Greater London), where he appears to have received the submission of Welsh rulers and northern earls.

Like both his elder brothers, Edred enjoyed military success over the Vikings. However, Edred was a strongly religious man with bad health (he had a stomach ailment and could barely eat). He never married or had children and brought up his murdered brother, Edmund's sons, Edwy and Edgar, as his heirs, and they both became king in turn.

He died on November 23, 955, at Frome in Somerset, and was buried at Winchester.

| | |
|---|---|
| Born: | c.923 |
| Parents: | Edward the Elder and Edgiva |
| House of: | Wessex |
| Became King: | May 26, 946 |
| Married: | Unmarried |
| Children: | None |
| Died: | November 23, 955 |
| Buried at: | Winchester |
| Succeeded by: | His nephew Edwy |

# 11.

# King Edwy
## "All-Fair"

Edmund I's elder son, Eadwig, also known as Edwy, was crowned by Oda, Archbishop of Canterbury, in 956 at Kingston-on-Thames.

Aged only 13 on his succession, Edwy became entangled in court factions, and Mercia & Northumbria broke away in rebellion. His short reign as King was marked by conflict. He had problems within his family, the Thanes, and the Roman Catholic Church, under the leadership of Saint Dunstan and Archbishop Odo. Edwy was also generous in making grants to the church and other religious institutions. He died before he was 20.

| | |
|---|---|
| Born: | c.940 |
| Parents: | Edmund and Elgiva |
| House of: | Wessex |
| Became King: | November 23, 955 |
| Married: | Ælgifu |
| Children: | None |
| Died: | October 1, 959 |
| Buried at: | Gloucester |
| Succeeded by: | His brother Edgar |

# King Edgar
## "The Peaceful"

RIGHT Detail of miniature from the New Minster Charter, 966, showing King Edgar flanked by the Virgin Mary and St Peter

Edgar was king in Mercia and the Danelaw from 957, and succeeded his brother as king of the English on Edwy's death in 959.

Edgar was a firm and capable ruler whose power was acknowledged by other rulers in Britain, as well as by Welsh and Scottish kings. Edgar's queen, Aelfthryth

| | |
|---|---|
| Born: | c.943 |
| Parents: | Edmund and Elgiva |
| House of: | Wessex |
| Became King: | October 1, 959 |
| Married: | (1) Ethelfleda, (2) Elfrida |
| Children: | 3 sons, 1 illegitimate daughter |
| Died: | July 8, 975 |
| Buried at: | Glastonbury |
| Succeeded by: | His son Edward |

was the first consort to be crowned queen of England.

Edgar was the patron of a great monastic revival which owed much to his association with Archbishop Dunstan. New bishoprics were created, Benedictine monasteries were reformed and old monastic sites were re-endowed with royal grants, some of which were of land recovered from the Vikings.

In the 970s and in the absence of Viking attacks, Edgar issued laws which for the first time dealt with Northumbria (parts of which were in the Danelaw) as well as Wessex and Mercia.

Edgar's coinage was uniform throughout the kingdom. A United Kingdom based on royal justice and order was emerging.

## KING EDGAR "THE PEACEFUL"

**LEFT** Silver 'Reform' penny of Edgar. Front showing Draped and diademed bust of Edgar within circle with words 'EADGAR REX ANGLOR'. Reverse small cross within circle with words 'LYFING MO NRÐPI'

# King Edward "The Martyr"

Elder son of King Edgar, he succeeded to the throne as a boy of 12, even though he was not his father's acknowledged heir. This aroused rival claims to the throne from his even younger half-brother, Ethelred II, the Unready.

| | |
|---|---|
| Born: | 963 |
| Parents: | Edgar and Ethelfreda |
| House of: | Wessex |
| Became King: | July 8, 975 |
| Married: | Unmarried |
| Children: | None |
| Died: | March 18, 978 |
| Buried at: | Wareham reburied Shaftesbury |
| Succeeded by: | His half brother Ethelred |

During King Edward's short reign, the opposition between the two political groups became more distinct. On one side were the former queen and her allies, who supported Prince Ethelred, and resisted the King and his policies. On the other side were King Edward and his advisors.

The King, still a teenager, was invited to the royal residence in Corfe, Dorset, where the young Prince and his mother were staying. As Edward approached, Ethelfreda's servants came out to greet him. Gathering around in apparent welcome, suddenly some of them seized his arms, and one of them plunged a dagger into his chest. Edward slumped from the saddle, and his horse bolted and raced into the woods near the castle. As Edward fell, his foot got caught in the stirrup, and the horrified onlookers saw the mortally wounded King dragged on the ground behind his horse. When the King's men finally reached and stopped the horse, Edward was dead. On the insistence of his mother, the body was buried without ceremony in the churchyard at Wareham, a few miles from the place it had fallen. He was about 15 years old. His body was reburied with great ceremony at Shaftesbury Abbey early in 980. In 1001 Edward's remains were moved to a more prominent place in the abbey, probably with the blessing of his half-brother King Ethelred. Edward was already thought a saint by this time.

# 14.

# King Ethelred II
## "The Unready"

RIGHT Silver penny of King Ethelred the unready

FAR RIGHT Depiction of King Ethelred II

The son of King Edgar and Queen Ælfthryth and was only about ten years old (no more than thirteen) when his half-brother Edward was murdered. Ethelred was not personally suspected of participation, but as the murder was committed at Corfe Castle by the attendants of Ælfthryth, it made it more difficult for the new king to rally the nation against the military raids by Danes, especially as the legend of St Edward the Martyr grew.

On 13 November 1002, Ethelred ordered the massacre of all Danish men in England on St Brice's Day. No

| | |
|---|---|
| Born: | c.968 |
| Parents: | Edgar and Elfrida |
| House of: | Wessex |
| Became King: | March 18, 978 |
| Married: | (1) Elfleda, (2) Emma |
| Children: | 9 sons, and 4 daughters |
| Died: | April 23, 1016 |
| Buried at: | St Paul's |
| Succeeded by: | His son Edmund |

order of this kind could be carried out in more than a third of England, where the Danes were too strong, but Gunhilde, sister of Sweyn Forkbeard, King of Denmark, was said to have been among the victims. It is likely that a wish to avenge her was a principal motive for Sweyn's invasion of western England the following year.. Sweyn then launched an invasion in 1013 intending to crown himself king of England, during which he proved himself to be a general greater than any other Viking leader of his generation. By the end of 1013 English resistance had collapsed and Sweyn had conquered the country, Ethelred II the Unready fled to Normandy in exile. He was recalled in 1014 on the death of Sweyn by leading English noblemen. Although crews of the Danish ships in the Trent that had supported Sweyn immediately swore their allegiance to Sweyn's son Canute.

War with Canute occupied the rest of Ethlelred's reign and over the next months Canute conquered most of England. Ethelred's son, Edmund, rejoined his father to defend London when Ethelred died on 23 April 1016.

The nickname "The Unready" is a corruption of the Old English 'unreed', meaning badly counselled or poorly advised.

# King Edmund II
## "Ironside"

After his father's death, the subsequent war between Edmund and Canute ended in a decisive victory for Canute at the Battle of Ashingdon on 18 October 1016.

Edmund's reputation as a warrior was such that Canute nevertheless agreed to divide England, Edmund taking Wessex and Canute the whole of the country beyond the Thames. However, Edmund died on 30 November and Canute became king of the whole country.

The nickname "Ironside" was for his staunch resistance to a massive invasion led by the Danish king Canute.

Edmund's two sons were reportedly sent by Canute to the king of Sweden to be murdered, but the king instead sent them to Hungary, where Edmund died and Edward prospered.

| | |
|---|---|
| Born: | c.990 |
| Parents: | Ethelred II and Elfleda |
| House of: | Wessex |
| Became King: | April 23, 1016 |
| Married: | Ealdgyth |
| Children: | 2 sons |
| Died: | November 30, 1016 |
| Buried at: | Glastonbury |
| Succeeded by: | Canute son of Sweyn who claimed the throne by conquest |

# King Canute

**K**ing of England from 1016, Denmark from 1018, and Norway from 1028.

Having invaded England in 1013 with his father, Sweyn, king of Denmark, he was acclaimed king on Sweyn's death in 1014 by his Viking army. Canute defeated Edmund (II) Ironside in 1016, and became king of all England on Edmund's death. He succeeded his brother Harold as king of Denmark in 1018, compelled King Malcolm to pay homage by invading Scotland in about 1027, and conquered Norway in 1028.

Under Canute's rule English trade improved, and he gained favour with his English subjects by sending soldiers back to Denmark. The legend of Canute disenchanting his flattering courtiers by showing that the sea would not retreat at his command was first told by Henry of Huntingdon in 1130 by saying that Canute set his throne by the sea shore and commanded the tide to halt and not wet his feet and robes. Yet "continuing

| Born: | c.995 in Denmark |
|---|---|
| Parents: | Sweyn I (Forkbeard) and Gunhilda |
| House of: | Denmark |
| Became King: | November 30, 1016 |
| Married: | (1) Emma of Normandy (2) Elfigfu |
| Children: | 3 sons, 1 daughter, and several illegitimate children |
| Died: | November 12, 1035 |
| Buried at: | Winchester |
| Succeeded by: | His son Harold |

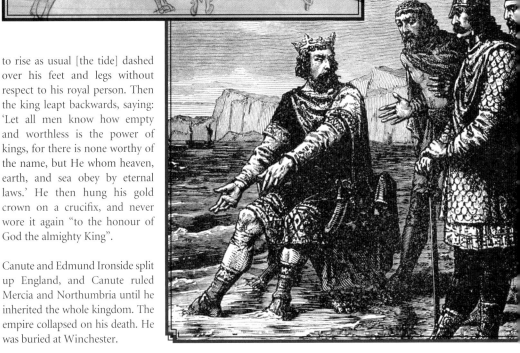

LEFT Medieval impression depicting Edmund Ironside (left) and Cnut (right)

to rise as usual [the tide] dashed over his feet and legs without respect to his royal person. Then the king leapt backwards, saying: 'Let all men know how empty and worthless is the power of kings, for there is none worthy of the name, but He whom heaven, earth, and sea obey by eternal laws.' He then hung his gold crown on a crucifix, and never wore it again "to the honour of God the almighty King".

Canute and Edmund Ironside split up England, and Canute ruled Mercia and Northumbria until he inherited the whole kingdom. The empire collapsed on his death. He was buried at Winchester.

# 17.

# King Harold I
## "Harefoot"

RIGHT The Life of King
Edward the Confessor,
13th century

MIDDLE A runestone in
Sweden which mentions
Harold Harefoot

FAR RIGHT Portrait
of King Harold I

He claimed the crown on the death of his father, when the rightful heir, his half-brother Harthacnut, was in Denmark and unable to ascend the throne.

He was elected king in 1037, but died three years later of a mysterious illness, as Harthacnut was preparing to invade England. The Nickname "Harefoot" referred to his speed and skill of huntsmanship

| | |
|---|---|
| Born: | c.1016 |
| Parents: | Canute and Elfigfu |
| House of: | Denmark |
| Became King: | November 12, 1035 |
| Married: | Unmarried |
| Children: | None |
| Died: | March 17, 1040 |
| Buried at: | Westminster reburied Southwark |
| Succeeded by: | His half brother Harthacnut |

# King Harthacnut
## (Canute III)

He was the eldest son of King Canute II and Emma of Normandy and was therefore the heir to the English crown. He had been proclaimed king of Denmark in 1028 but when Canute died in 1035 Harthacnut was defending his land in Denmark.

In his absence his half-brother, Harold Harefoot was crowned King Harold I of England in 1037. Naturally there was a struggle between the two brothers

| | |
|---|---|
| Born: | c.1018 |
| Parents: | Canute and Emma of Normandy |
| House of: | Denmark |
| Became King: | March 17, 1040 |
| Married: | Unmarried |
| Children: | None |
| Died: | June 8, 1042 |
| Buried at: | Winchester |
| Succeeded by: | His half brother Edward |

that only ended on the death of Harold (17 June 1040). Harthacnut sailed to England with a large fleet and was immediately accepted as king.

On 8 June 1042, Harthacnut attended a wedding. Harthacnut presumably consumed large quantities of alcohol. As he was drinking to the health of the bride, he "died as he stood at his drink, and he suddenly fell to the earth with an awful convulsion; and those who were close by took hold of him, and he spoke no word afterwards"

He was succeeded by Magnus in Denmark and Edward the Confessor in England.

Harthacnut was the last Danish king to rule England.

ABOVE Depiction of Harthacnut meeting King Magnus

## 19.

# King Edward
## "The Confessor"

King of England from 1042, the son of Ethelred II. Edward was known as 'the Confessor' because of his deep piety. He lived in Normandy with his mother Emma of Normandy's relatives until shortly before his accession to the English Throne. According to those who compiled the Anglo-Saxon Chronicle, the first thing Edward did, despite his religious views, was to deprive his mother of all of her estates and reduce her to relative poverty. It is said that Edward blamed her for his miserable and lonely childhood.

Edward married in 1045. His wife, Edith, was the daughter of Godwin of Wessex, the most important nobleman in England. They had no children as Edward had taken a vow of celibacy.

During his reign power was held by Earl Godwin and his son Harold, while the king devoted himself to religion and in his final years Edward was occupied with rebuilding the abbey church of St. Peter

| | |
|---|---|
| Born: | c.1004 at Islip |
| Parents: | Ethelred II and Emma of Normandy |
| House of: | Wessex |
| Became King: | June 8, 1042 |
| Married: | Edith, Daughter of Earl Godwin of Wessex |
| Children: | None |
| Died: | January 5, 1066 |
| Buried at: | Westminster Abbey |
| Succeeded by: | His brother-in-law Harold |

at Westminster, but by the time it was consecrated (December 1065) he was too ill to attend.

Edward died in January 1066 and his childlessness led to a struggle for power. The succession went first to Harold and then to the conquest by William of Normandy nine months later at the Battle of Hastings in October 1066. Edward was canonized in 1161.

Edward was one of the last Anglo-Saxon kings of England and is usually regarded as the last king of the House of Wessex, ruling from 1042 to 1066

# King Harold II

King Harold II was the last Anglo-Saxon king of England. Harold succeeded his father Earl Godwine in 1053 as Earl of Wessex..

| | |
|---|---|
| Born: | c.1020 |
| Parents: | Godwin, Earl of Wessex, and Gytha of Denmark |
| House of: | Wessex |
| Became King: | January 5, 1066 |
| Married: | (1) Eadgyth, Daughter of Earl of Mercia (2) Ealdyth widow of Gruffydd ap Llywelyn |
| Children: | 1 or 2 sons and several illegitimate children |
| Died: | October 14, 1066 |
| Buried at: | Pevensey reburied Waltham Abbey |
| Succeeded by: | Edgar the Aethling, and then William of Normandy |

He had no bloodline to the throne but his sister Edith was married to King Edward the Confessor. In January 1066 when Edward died childless, the Witan (or Witenagemot a council of high-ranking religious and secular men) elected Harold to succeed him and one day later he was crowned King Harold II. William of Normandy claimed that he had been promised the throne by his relative Edward and that in 1063 Harold had sworn allegiance to support his claim. On hearing of Harold's coronation William prepared to invade England to claim the throne.

Meanwhile, Harold's brother Tostig who had quarrelled with Harold joined the king of Norway Harald Hardrada in invading Northumbria. Harold routed

and killed them at Stamford Bridge, near York, on 25 September. Harold then heard that William had landed 250 miles to the south, and he gathered his troops and marched south in 11 days. The Battle of Hastings took place on 14 October 1066.

Harold's army was defeated and he was killed in the battle. From evidence of the Bayeux Tapestry (made about 1077) he was either shot in the eye with an arrow or had his legs hacked from under him by a Norman foot soldier.

# King William I
## "The Conqueror"

**RIGHT** Portrait of King William I "The Conqueror"

He was the first Norman King of England. The descendant of Viking raiders, he had been Duke of Normandy since 1035.

| Born: | September 1028 at Falaise, Normandy |
|---|---|
| Parents: | Robert I, Duke of Normandy, and Arlette daughter of Fulbert (illegitimate) |
| House of: | Normandy |
| Became King: | December 25, 1066 aged 38 years |
| Married: | Matilda, Daughter of Count of Flanders |
| Children: | 4 sons , and 6 daughters |
| Died: | September 9, 1087 |
| Buried at: | St Stephens Abbey, Caen, Normandy |
| Succeeded by: | His son William II |

William's coronation took place in Westminster Abbey on Christmas Day 1066. William ordered the compilation of the Domesday Book, a survey listing all the landholders in England along with their holdings.

In 1051 Edward the Confessor had nominated William as heir to the English throne, but when he died in January 1066 Harold (II) Godwinson was crowned. William immediately began preparations for an invasion of England. On 28 September his forces landed unopposed at Pevensey, Sussex. Harold was in the north of England defeating an invasion led by Harald Hardrada, King of Norway, but immediately marched south to meet William. Their armies clashed in the Battle of Hastings on 14 October 1066. Harold was slain and William achieved a decisive victory. In 1067 William forcibly brought southwest England under his control.

In 1068 he marched north and east to establish a number of strategic fortifications. In the summer of 1069 Swein Estrithson of Denmark landed with a considerable force in the Humber and was welcomed by the northern English earls who joined him in expelling the Norman garrison at York. William immediately marched north, destroying everything in his path, and reoccupied York. He undertook a systematic harrying of the north, setting his troops to kill and burn in order to leave nothing that could support future rebellion. The Danish fleet was bought off and departed. In 1072 William led an invasion that forced King Malcolm of Scotland to surrender hostages and swear loyalty. In 1073 he was back in France suppressing rebellion in Maine. His regents dealt with a rebellion by the English earls in 1075, and in the latter years of his reign, William twice faced rebellion in Normandy led by his eldest son, Robert Curthose. In 1087 William sacked the French-controlled town of Nantes in the Vexin. In the fighting he suffered a fatal internal injury after being thrown against the pommel of his saddle. He was

taken to the priory of Saint-Gervais near Rouen. Before he died, William was ill for some weeks and had time to repent. He reputedly confessed his brutality saying "I am stained with the rivers of blood that I have spilled"

# King William II
## "Rufus"

King of England from 1087, the third son of William (I) the Conqueror. William is commonly known as William Rufus or William the Red, perhaps because of his red-faced appearance.

| | |
|---|---|
| Born: | c.1056 at Normandy |
| Parents: | William I and Matilda of Flanders |
| House of: | Normandy |
| Became King: | September 9, 1087 |
| Married: | Unmarried |
| Children: | None |
| Died: | August 2, 1100 |
| Buried at: | Winchester |
| Succeeded by: | His brother Henry |

He spent most of his reign attempting to capture Normandy from his brother Robert (II) Curthose , Duke of Normandy. His extortion of money led his barons to revolt. Malcolm II of Scotland twice invaded England in 1091 and 1093 before Malcolm was defeated and killed at the Battle of Alnwick. William also had to deal with rebellions in Northumbria and along the Welsh border.

William died in suspicious circumstances. He went hunting on 2 August 1100 in the New Forest, probably near Brockenhurst, and was killed by an arrow through the lung. The king's body was abandoned by the nobles at the place where he fell. A peasant later found it.

# King Henry I

The youngest son of William the Conqueror, he succeeded his brother William II. He won the support of the Saxons by granting them a charter and marrying a Saxon princess, Edith, daughter of Malcolm III of Scotland.

| | |
|---|---|
| Born: | September, 1068 at Selby, Yorkshire |
| Parents: | William I and Matilda of Flanders |
| House of: | Normandy |
| Became King: | August 3, 1100 |
| Married: | (1) Edith (Matilda), (2) Adelicia |
| Children: | 1 daughter and 1 son, and many illegitimate children |
| Died: | December 2, 1135 |
| Buried at: | Reading |
| Succeeded by: | His nephew Stephen |

She was known as Matilda after her marriage, a name more acceptable to the Norman Barons than her Saxon name Edith. Henry's daughter was also called Matilda. He was an able administrator, and established a professional bureaucracy and a system of travelling judges. He was called Beauclerc because of his scholarly interests.

In 1101 his elder brother Robert, Duke of Normandy, attempted to seize the crown by invading England. However, after the Treaty of Alton, Robert agreed to recognise his brother Henry as King and returned to Normandy. They fought again in 1106 at Battle of Tinchebrai at which Robert was captured and Henry became Duke of Normandy as well as King of England. In November 1120,

Henry's son, William, died in a shipwreck and from then on the question of the succession dominated the politics of the reign. Henry summoned his only other legitimate child Matilda, back to England and made his barons pay homage to her as his heir. In 1128, Matilda was married to Geoffrey Plantagenet. English barons did not want to be ruled by a woman and on Henry's death in December 1135, there was a succession crisis which led to civil war.

Henry died in Normandy in 1135 of food poisoning according to legend from overeating on lampreys (an eel type fish).

# King Stephen

RIGHT King Stephen's bones may be under a school in Faversham, Kent.

King of England from 1135. A grandson of William the Conqueror, he was elected king in 1135, although he had previously recognized Henry I's daughter Matilda as heiress to the throne. Matilda landed in England in 1139, and civil war disrupted the country with fighting between Stephen and forces loyal to Matilda. Stephen was briefly taken prisoner and Matilda declared Queen until she was defeated at the Battle of Faringdon in 1145.

| | |
|---|---|
| Born: | c.1097 at Blois, France |
| Parents: | Stephen, Count of Blois, and Adela (daughter of William I) |
| House of: | Blois |
| Became King: | December 22, 1135 |
| Married: | Matilda, Daughter of Eustace III, Count of Boulogne |
| Children: | 3 sons and 2 daughters, plus at least 5 illegitimate children |
| Died: | October 25, 1154 |
| Buried at: | Faversham, Kent |
| Succeeded by: | Henry II |

Although Stephen and other nobles pledged to support Henry's daughter, Matilda, as Henry's successor there was widespread unhappiness at the thought of a woman ruler. Consequently, after Henry I died in December 1135, the leading lords and bishops welcomed Stephen as the new king. He was not a natural leader, rapidly making concessions that exposed his weakness. He appointed large numbers of new earls, an expensive act that brought little reward and alienated

ABOVE Matilda of Boulogne, King Stephen's wife

his nobles with his desperate measures to build support and with the lawlessness of his Flemish mercenaries.

In 1138, Matilda's half brother, Robert, Earl of Gloucester, took up arms on her behalf. Early victories for Stephen faded when he lost the support of the church. Seizing her opportunity, Matilda invaded England in September 1139. Stephen had Matilda escorted to Bristol, whereupon she proceeded to take control of western England. Early in 1141, Matilda's supporters captured Stephen in a battle at Lincoln. In November, he was exchanged for Gloucester, who had been captured by forces loyal to the king. Over time, Stephen gained the upper hand and in 1148 Matilda left England.

Stephen hoped to secure the succession for his son, Eustace, but to do so he had to deal with Matilda's son, Henry of Anjou, who invaded England in January 1153 to claim his royal inheritance. When Eustace died in August, Stephen lost heart; he signed a treaty designating Henry as his successor. At Stephen's death, Henry ascended the throne as King Henry II.

# King Henry II

RIGHT 12th-century depiction of Henry and Eleanor holding court

FAR RIGHT Portrait of King Henry II

The first Plantagenet King, Henry succeeded his cousin King Stephen. He was an energetic and sometimes ruthless ruler, driven by a desire to restore the lands and privileges of his royal grandfather, Henry I.

| | |
|---|---|
| Born: | March 5, 1133 at Le Mans, France |
| Parents: | Geoffrey, Count of Anjou, and Empress Matilda |
| House of: | Angevin |
| Became King: | October 25, 1154 |
| Married: | Eleanor of Aquitaine, Daughter of William X, Duke of Aquitaine |
| Children: | 5 sons, 3 daughters and several illegitimate children |
| Died: | July 6, 1189 |
| Buried at: | Fontevraud, France |
| Succeeded by: | His son Richard |

Henry was lord of Scotland, Ireland, and Wales, and Count of Anjou, Brittany, Poitou, Normandy, Maine, and Gascony. He claimed Aquitaine through marriage to the heiress Eleanor in 1152.

Henry's many French possessions caused him to live for more than half his reign outside England. This made it essential for him to establish a judicial and administrative system which would work during his absence.

For the first ten years of his reign Henry and Thomas a Becket, England's leading prelate, were close friends. Thomas was then persuaded to become archbishop of

Canterbury in 1162 in the hope that he would help the king curb the power of the ecclesiastical courts. However, once consecrated, Becket felt bound to defend church privileges, and he was murdered in Canterbury Cathedral 1170 by four knights of the king's household.

In 1171 Henry invaded Ireland and received homage from the King of Leinster. Henry also had problems within his own family. His sons - Henry, Geoffrey, Richard and John - mistrusted each other and resented their father's policy of dividing land among them

Henry was succeeded by his son Richard (I) the Lionheart

# King Richard I
## "The Lion Heart"

**RIGHT** Effigy
(c. 1199) of Richard I at
Fontevraud
Abbey, Anjou

**RIGHT** Effigy
(c. 1199) of Richard I at
Fontevraud
Abbey, Anjou

**FAR RIGHT** Depiction
of King Richard I

Richard was the third son of Henry II. He twice rebelled against his father before he became King of England in 1189, but based himself in his Duchy in Aquitaine inherited from his mother Eleanor. He spent only six months of his reign in England and spoke only French. He appointed William Longchamps, Bishop of Ely, as Chancellor of England during his absence but he was overthrown by Richard's brother John.

| | |
|---|---|
| Born: | September 6, 1157 at Beaumont Place, Oxford |
| Parents: | Henry II and Eleanor of Aquitaine |
| House of: | Angevin |
| Became King: | July 6, 1189 |
| Married: | Berengaria, Daughter of Sancho V of Navarre |
| Children: | 2 illegitimate sons |
| Died: | April 6, 1199 |
| Buried at: | Fontevraud, France |
| Succeeded by: | His brother John |

Richard acquired a reputation as a leader and warrior becoming known as Richard 'The Lion Heart' or 'Coeur de Lion'. His experience in warfare came from controlling rebellions in Poitou in the 1170s and against his father, Henry II, in 1183. He took up Henry's plans to recover Jerusalem on his accession in 1189 and set out to establish bases for crusades in Sicily in 1190 and Cyprus, which he took in 1191. Engaging in the siege of Acre, which he brought to a swift conclusion, he set off down the coast to Jaffa, conducting a fighting march against Saladin.

In the third Crusade 1191–92 he won victories at Cyprus, Acre, and Arsuf (against Saladin), but failed to recover Jerusalem. While returning overland he was captured by the Duke of Austria, who handed him over to the emperor Henry VI. He was held prisoner until a large ransom was raised.

On his release he returned briefly to England, where his brother John had been ruling in his stead. His later years were spent in warfare in France, where he was killed by a crossbow bolt while besieging Châlus-Chabrol in 1199. He left no heir.

# King John

John was nicknamed Lackland, probably because, as the youngest of Henry II's five sons, it was difficult to find a portion of his father's French possessions for him to inherit. He was acting king from 1189 during his brother Richard the Lion-Heart's absence on the Third Crusade. The legend of Robin Hood dates from this time in which John is portrayed as Bad King John. He was involved in intrigues against his absent brother, but became king in 1199 when Richard was killed in battle in France.

| | |
|---|---|
| Born: | December 24, 1166 at Beaumont Palace : Oxford |
| Parents: | Henry II and Eleanor of Aquitaine |
| House of: | Angevin |
| Became King: | April 6, 1199 |
| Married: | 1) Isabella of Gloucester, (annulled 1199), (2) Isabella, Daughter of Count of Angouleme |
| Children: | 2 sons, 3 daughters and several illegitimate children |
| Died: | October 18, 1216 |
| Buried at: | Worcester |
| Succeeded by: | His son Henry III |

Most of his reign was dominated by war with France. John had lost Normandy and almost all the other English possessions in France to Philip II of France by 1204. He spent the next decade trying to regain these without success and was finally defeated by Philip Augustus at the Battle of Bouvines in 1214. He was also in conflict with the Church. In 1205 he disputed the pope's choice of Stephen

Langton as archbishop of Canterbury, and Pope Innocent III placed England under an interdict, suspending all religious services, including baptisms, marriages, and burials. John retaliated by seizing church revenues, and in 1209 was excommunicated. Eventually, John submitted, accepting the papal nominee, and agreed to hold the kingdom as a fief of the papacy; an annual monetary tribute was paid to the popes for the next 150 years by successive English monarchs.

His repressive policies and ruthless taxation to fund the war in France brought him into conflict with his barons which became known as the Barons War. In 1215 a revolt by leading barons forced John to agree to a charter of liberties. Their demands were drawn up in a document which became the known as the Magna Carta (Great Charter). John met them at Runnymede where on 15th June 1215 he agreed to their demands and sealed the Magna Carta. It was a remarkable document which set limits on the powers of the king, laid out the feudal obligations of the barons, confirmed the liberties of the Church, and granted rights to all freemen of the realm and their heirs for ever.

His concessions did not buy peace for long and the Barons War continued. The barons sought French aid and Prince Louis of France landed in England supported by attacks from the North by Alexander II of Scotland. John fled and according to legend lost most of his baggage and the crown jewels when crossing the tidal estuaries of the Wash. He became ill with dysentery and died at Newark Castle in October 1216.

BELOW King John "Lackland"

# King Henry III

He became king when he was only 9 years old, succeeding his father, John, but the royal powers were exercised by a regency until 1232, and by two French nobles, Peter des Roches and Peter des Rivaux, until the barons forced their expulsion in 1234, marking the start of Henry's personal rule.

Henry married the beautiful 19-year

| | |
|---|---|
| Born: | October 1, 1207 at Winchester |
| Parents: | King John and Isabella of Angouleme |
| House of: | Plantagenet |
| Became King: | October 18, 1216 |
| Married: | Eleanor of Provence, Daughter of Raymond Berenger |
| Children: | 6 sons and 3 daughters |
| Died: | November 16, 1272 |
| Buried at: | Westminster Abbey |
| Succeeded by: | His son Edward |

ABOVE Effigy of
King Henry III in
Westminster Abbey

old Eleanor of Provence in Canterbury Cathedral in January 1236. He renovated the royal palace at Westminster installing glass in the windows and plumbing.

Henry built a menagerie at the Tower of London – mainly to house an elephant that was a gift from France's King Louis IX. Henry was also gifted a polar bear from the King of Norway.

His financial commitments to the papacy and his foreign favourites antagonized the barons who issued the Provisions of Oxford in 1258, limiting the king's power. Henry's refusal to accept the provisions led to the second Barons' War in 1264, a revolt of nobles led by his brother-in-law Simon de Montfort. Henry was defeated at Lewes, Sussex, and imprisoned, but restored to the throne after the royalist victory at Evesham in 1265.

On his release Henry was weak and senile and his eldest son, Edward, took charge of the government.

# 29

# King Edward I
## "Longshanks"

Edward was nicknamed "Long-shanks" due to his great height and stature.

| | |
|---|---|
| Born: | June 17, 1239 |
| Parents: | Henry III ad Eleanor of Provence |
| House of: | Plantagenet |
| Became King: | November 20, 1272 |
| Crowned: | August 19, 1274 at Westminster Abbey |
| Married: | (1) Eleanor, Daughter of Ferdinand III of Castile, (2) Margaret, Daughter of Philip III of France |
| Children: | 6 sons and 12 daughters |
| Died: | July 7, 1307 |
| Buried at: | Westminster Abbey |
| Succeeded by: | His son Edward II |

He led the royal forces against Simon de Montfort (the Younger) in the Barons' War of 1264–67, and was on a crusade when he succeeded to the throne. His reign saw Parliament move towards its modern form with the Model Parliament of 1295. He married Eleanor of Castile (1254–90) and in 1299 married Margaret, daughter of Philip III of France.

Edward was a noted castle builder, including the northern Welsh Conway castle, Caernarvon castle, Beaumaris castle, and Harlech castle. He was also responsible for building bastides to defend the English position in France.

In 1292, Edward was asked to arbitrate in a succession dispute in Scotland and

**LEFT** Portrait in Westminster Abbey, thought to be of Edward I

nominated John Balliol as king. Balliol duly swore allegiance to Edward, but Edward's demands pushed the Scots into an alliance with France.

Edward invaded and conquered Scotland. Opposition gathered around William Wallace, but he was captured by the English and executed in 1305. In 1306, the Scottish nobleman Robert the Bruce rebelled.

Edward was on his way to fight Bruce when he died, on 7 July 1307.

# 30

# King Edward II

Born at Caernarvon Castle, Edward II was created the first Prince of Wales in 1301.

Before he became king, Edward's close and probably homosexual relationship with Piers Gaveston caused scandal at

| | |
|---|---|
| Born: | April 25, 1284 at Caernarvon, Wales |
| Parents: | Edward I and Eleanor of Castile |
| House of: | Plantagenet |
| Became King: | July 8, 1307 |
| Crowned: | February 25, 1308 at Westminster Abbey |
| Married: | Isabella, Daughter of Philip IV of France |
| Children: | 2 sons and 2 daughters |
| Died: | September 21, 1327 |
| Buried at: | Gloucester |
| Succeeded by: | His son Edward III |

court. When he became king, Edward made Gaveston Earl of Cornwall. Leading barons led by Thomas Earl of Lancaster turned against Edward and he was forced to agree to a series of demands which among other things required him to strip Gaveston of his title and send him to exile. However, after a year Gaveston returned. The angry barons seized him and at Blacklow Hill in Warwickshire they beheaded him.

His invasion of Scotland in 1314 to suppress revolt resulted in defeat at Bannockburn. When he fell under the influence of a new favourite, Hugh le Depenser, he was deposed in 1327 by his wife Isabella, daughter of Philip IV of France, and her lover Roger de Mortimer, and murdered in Berkeley Castle, Gloucestershire.

He was succeeded by his son, Edward III

FAR LEFT Covered-walkway leading to a cell within Berkeley Castle, by tradition associated with Edward's imprisonment

TOP LEFT Portrait of King Edward II

TOP RIGHT Tomb of Edward II in Gloucester Cathedral

# King Edward III

Edward became king in 1327 after his father was deposed by his mother and her lover, Roger Mortimer.

| Born: | November 13, 1312 at Windsor Castle |
|---|---|
| Parents: | Edward II and Isabella of France |
| House of: | Plantagenet |
| Became King: | January 25, 1327 |
| Married: | Philippa, Daughter of Count of Hainault |
| Children: | 7 sons and 5 daughters, plus at least 3 illegitimate |
| Died: | June 21, 1377 |
| Buried at: | Westminster Abbey |
| Succeeded by: | His grandson Richard II |

A year later Edward married Philippa of Hainault. His mother, Isabella, and Roger Mortimer ruled in Edward's name until 1330, when he executed Mortimer and banished his mother.

He assumed the government in 1330 from his mother, through whom in 1337 he laid claim to the French throne and thus began the Hundred Years' War. Edward was the victor of Halidon Hill in 1333, Sluys in 1340, Crécy in 1346, and at the siege of Calais 1346–47, and created the Order of the Garter.

Edward's early experience was against the Scots, including the disastrous Weardale campaign in 1327. Forcing them to battle outside Berwick at Halidon Hill he used a combination of dismounted men-at-

arms and archers to crush the Scots. Apart from the naval victory of Sluys his initial campaigns against France were expensive and inconclusive. Resorting to chevauchée (raids through enemy territory), he scored a stunning victory at Crécy, which delivered the crucial bridgehead of Calais into English hands. Due to the brilliant success of his son Edward of Woodstock (Edward the Black Prince) at Poitiers in 1356, and later campaigns, Edward achieved the Treaty of Brétigny in 1360. He gave up personal command in the latter part of his reign.

Edward formed the Order of The Garter, a chivalric club consisting of 26 knights, the King and Prince of Wales and 12 companions and was designed to bind his military nobility to him.

The Black Death hit England in 1348 and Princess Joan, the King's favourite daughter was one of it's victims.

Edward died on 21 June 1377, leaving his young grandson Richard as king

**ABOVE** Edward III as he was portrayed in the late 16th century

# King Richard II

RIGHT Coat of Arms of
King Richard II

FAR RIGHT Richard II
Coronation portrait

King of England from 1377, effectively from 1389, son of Edward the Black Prince. He reigned in conflict with Parliament; they executed some of his associates in 1388, and he executed some of the opposing barons in 1397, whereupon he made himself absolute.

| | |
|---|---|
| Born: | January 6, 1367 at Bordeaux, France |
| Parents: | Edward, the Black Prince, and Joan of Kent |
| House of: | Plantagenet |
| Became King: | June 22, 1377 |
| Married: | (1) Anne of Bohemia, (2) Isabella, nine year old daughter of Charles VI of France |
| Children: | None |
| Died: | February 14, 1400 |
| Buried at: | Langley reburied Westminster |
| Succeeded by: | His cousin Henry IV |

In 1381 Richard was faced with the Peasants' Revolt, a result of the imposition of the Poll Tax in 1380. The leader of the Revolt, Wat Tyler, was stabbed and killed at Smithfield by the Lord Mayor of London, fearing for the safety of the king. The young King Richard showed apparent courage in facing the mobs gathered at Mile End and Smithfield and also contributed to the failure of the uprising.

Richard was born in Bordeaux. His fondness for favourites resulted in conflicts with Parliament, and in 1388 the baronial party, headed by the Duke of Gloucester, had many of his friends executed. Richard recovered control in 1389, and ruled until 1397, when he had Gloucester murdered and his other leading opponents executed or banished, and assumed absolute power.

In 1399 his cousin Henry Bolingbroke, Duke of Hereford (later Henry IV), returned from exile to lead a revolt.

Two years later, forced to abdicate in favour of Henry IV, Richard was imprisoned in Pontefract Castle, where he died possibly of starvation.

# King Henry IV

RIGHT The tomb of
Henry IV and his 2nd
wife, Joan of Navarre,
in Canterbury Cathedral

FAR RIGHT 16th
century painting of
Henry IV

As king, Henry's first task was to strengthen his position. Most rebellions were quashed easily, but the revolt of the Welsh squire Owen Glendower in 1400 was more serious. In 1403, Glendower allied himself with Henry Percy, Earl of Northumberland, and his son Henry, called Hotspur. Hotspur's brief uprising, Henry's most serious challenge, ended when he was defeated and killed in the Battle of Shrewsbury in July 1403.

| | |
|---|---|
| Born: | April 4, 1366 at Bolingbroke Castle, Lincolnshire |
| Parents: | John of Gaunt and Blanche of Lancaster |
| House of: | Lancaster |
| Became King: | September 30, 1399 |
| Married: | (1) Mary de Bohun, (2) Joan, Daughter of Charles II of Navarre |
| Children: | 5 sons and 2 daughters |
| Died: | March 20, 1413 |
| Buried at: | Canterbury |
| Succeeded by: | His son Henry V |

Northumberland's subsequent rebellion was quickly suppressed and the rebel army suffered a decisive defeat at the Battle of Bramham Moor, after which Northumberland was executed.

The later years of Henry's reign were marked by serious health problems. He had a disfiguring skin disease likened to leprosy. A power struggle developed between his favourite, Thomas

Arundel, Archbishop of Canterbury, and a faction headed by Henry's half brothers and his son, Prince Henry.

Arguments raged over the best strategy to take in France, where civil war had erupted. Prince Henry wanted to resume war in France, but the king favoured peace.

Uneasy relations between the prince and his father persisted until Henry's death.

# King Henry V

**RIGHT** King Henry V's wife, Catherine of Valois, Queen of England

**FAR RIGHT** Warrior king – Henry had a soldier's haircut

Henry was determined to regain the lands in France held by his ancestors and laid claim to the French throne. He captured the port of Harfleur and on 25 October 1415 defeated the French at the Battle of Agincourt – with a small army of only 6,000 men. This battle proved to be one of the most famous military exploits in English history.

| | |
|---|---|
| Born: | August 9, 1387 at Monmouth Castle |
| Parents: | Henry IV and Mary de Bohun |
| House of: | Lancaster |
| Became King: | March 20, 1413 |
| Married: | Catherine de Valois |
| Children: | 1 son |
| Died: | August 31, 1422 |
| Buried at: | Westminster |
| Succeeded by: | His son Henry VI |

Between 1417 and 1419 Henry followed up with another campaign and captured Caen and Rouen, capital of Normandy. Henry then married the French King, Charles VI's daughter Catherine and under the Treaty of Troyes was recognised as heir to the French throne.

In February 1421, Henry returned to England to great acclaim by his subjects who reportedly shouted "Welcome, Henry V King of England and France" as he and his Queen rode through London. Queen Catherine gave birth to their son, Henry, on 6 December 1421.

Almost a year later Henry V died suddenly on 31 August 1422 near Paris, apparently from dysentery, which he had contracted during the siege of Meaux. He was almost 36 years old.

Shortly before his death, Henry V had named his brother John, Duke of Bedford, regent of France in the name of his son Henry VI, then only a few months old. Henry V was never crowned King of France himself, as he might have expected after the Treaty of Troyes, because Charles VI, to whom he had been named heir, survived him by two months.

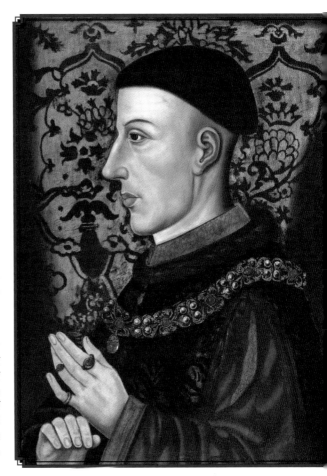

# King Henry VI

RIGHT Henry VI and
Margaret of Anjou

FAR RIGHT Portrait
of Henry VI

Henry VI became king at the age of only 9 months and just two months later on the death of King Charles VI of France he became King of France, although disputed. The youngest ever King of England, his father had appointed his uncle, Duke Humphrey of Gloucester to act as regent, but he was soon opposed by Henry Beaufort, Bishop of Winchester and Chancellor of England.

Henry assumed royal power 1442 and sided with the party opposed to the continuation of the Hundred Years' War with France. Unlike his father, Henry was disinclined to warfare, and when Joan of Arc revived French patriotism the English gradually began to lose their French possessions. By 1453 only Calais remained of his father's conquests.

Henry had periods of insanity and his wife, Margaret of Anjou took control.

| | |
|---|---|
| Born: | December 6, 1421 at Windsor Castle |
| Parents: | Henry V and Catherine of Valois |
| House of: | Lancaster |
| Became King: | September 1, 1422 |
| Married: | Margaret, Daughter of Count of Anjou |
| Children: | One son |
| Died: | May 21, 1471 |
| Buried at: | Chertsey, reburied in 1485 when his body was moved to St George's Chapel, Windsor Castle. |
| Succeeded by: | His distant cousin Edward IV |

However, he eventually was deposed 1461 in the Wars of the Roses by Edward of York – who then became king. Henry hid in Scotland but was captured in1465 and imprisoned in the Tower of London – his Queen exiled in Scotland and then France before helping to restore Henry VI to the throne in October 1470. However, by this time, years in hiding followed by years in captivity had taken their toll on him and his return to the throne only lasted about 6 months before Edward IV regained the throne - The Yorkists won a final decisive victory at the Battle of Tewkesbury on 4 May 1471, where Henry's only son Edward was killed.

Henry died in the Tower of London some say from melancholy upon hearing of his son's death, but some say he was murdered on the instruction of Edward IV.

# King Edward IV

RIGHT Elizabeth
Woodville – who
Edward married secretly
in May 1464

FAR RIGHT Edward IV
was 6ft 4in tall and was
powerfully built

After his father's death Edward occupied London in 1461, and was proclaimed king in place of Henry VI by a council of peers. His position was secured by the defeat of the Lancastrians at Towton and by the capture of Henry.

He quarrelled, however, with Richard Neville, Earl of Warwick, his strongest supporter, who in 1470 betrayed him and helped to temporarily restore Henry, forcing Edward into exile - until Edward recovered the throne after defeating and killing Warwick in battle at Barnet.

| | |
|---|---|
| Born: | April 28, 1442 at Rouen, France |
| Parents: | Richard, Duke of York, and Cecily Neville |
| House of: | York |
| Became King: | March 4, 1461 |
| Married: | Elizabeth, Daughter of Richard Woodville |
| Children: | 3 sons, 7 daughters and 4 illegitimate children |
| Died: | April 9, 1483 |
| Buried at: | Windsor |
| Succeeded by: | His son Edward V |

Edward had a reputation of being a womaniser early in his reign and his weakness for beautiful women led to his secret marriage to Elizabeth Woodville who was a widow of a Lancastrian sympathiser.

Edward's two younger brothers, George and Richard (later King Richard III), both married daughters of Warwick. In 1478, George was found guilty of plotting against

Edward. He was imprisoned in the Tower of London and privately executed - according to a long standing belief he was "drowned in a butt of Malmsey wine".

Edward did not face any further rebellions, as the Lancastrian line had practically been extinguished, and the only contender left was Henry Tudor, who was living in exile.

Edward was a man of culture as well as a warrior and political plotter – during his reign William Caxton printed the first dated book in English, which was financed by the King.

Edward was also known for his over indulgence which it is believed could have attributed to his death possibly from pneumonia or a stroke in 1483.

# King Edward V

King of England 1483 for just 86 days.

Edward was never crowned and was deposed three months after his accession in favour of his uncle and Lord Protector, Richard, Duke of Gloucester (Richard III). Gloucester had Edward and his brother Richard housed in the Tower of London (which was a palace as well as a prison). Soon afterwards, Richard Duke of Gloucester became King and the princes were never seen again. It is traditionally believed the two boys were murdered on Richard's orders.

| | |
|---|---|
| Born: | November 4, 1470 at Westminster |
| Parents: | Edward IV and Elizabeth Woodville |
| House of: | York |
| Became King: | April 9, 1483 |
| Crowned: | Not crowned |
| Married: | Unmarried |
| Children: | None |
| Died: | September, 1483 |
| Buried at: | Tower of London |
| Succeeded by: | His uncle Richard III |

# King Richard III

RIGHT Richard III was the first monarch to swear the Coronation Oath in English

Cruelly nicknamed "Crookback" by some because of a curvature of his spine that developed in his youth, the son of Richard, Duke of York, was created Duke of Gloucester by his brother Edward IV, and distinguished himself in the Wars of the Roses.

| | |
|---|---|
| Born: | October 2, 1452 at Fotheringhay Castle |
| Parents: | Richard, Duke of York and Cecily Neville |
| House of: | York |
| Became King: | June 26, 1483 |
| Married: | Anne Neville, widow of Edward, Prince of Wales and daughter of Earl of Warwick |
| Children: | 1 son, plus several illegitimate children before his marriage |
| Died: | August 22, 1485 |
| Buried at: | Leicester |
| Succeeded by: | His distant cousin Henry VII |

On Edward's death 1483 he became protector to his nephew Edward V, and soon secured the crown for himself stating that Edward IV's sons were illegitimate because his marriage was illegal. It has always been widely presumed that he ordered the murder of his two nephews in the Tower of London, which undermined his popularity.

In 1485 Henry, Earl of Richmond (later Henry VII), raised a rebellion, and Richard III was defeated and killed at Bosworth. After Richard's death on the battlefield his rival was crowned King Henry VII and became the first English monarch of the Tudor dynasty.

Richard was the last English king to die in battle. His body was taken to Leicester where it was buried at Greyfriars Church in a Franciscan Friary which was subsequently destroyed during the Dissolution of the Monasteries 1536 to 1541.

In September 2012 archeologists uncovered remains of the church buried underneath a car park and found a skeleton of an adult male showing severe scoliosis of the spine, a major head wound, and an arrowhead lodged in his spine. On 12 September it was announced that the skeleton discovered during the search might be that of Richard III.

On 4 Feb 2013 experts announced that DNA from the bones matched that of descendants of the king's family. A leading archaeologist said: "Beyond reasonable doubt it's Richard." There are plans to have his remains re-buried in Leicester cathedral.

# King Henry VII

Henry was the first of the Tudor monarchs. His father, Edmund Tudor, Earl of Richmond, died before he was born, and his mother,

| | |
|---|---|
| Born: | January 28, 1457 at Pembroke Castle |
| Parents: | Edmund Tudor, Earl of Richmond, and Margaret Beaufort |
| House of: | Tudor |
| Became King: | August 22, 1485 |
| Married: | Elizabeth of York, daughter of Edward IV |
| Children: | 3 sons and 4 daughters |
| Died: | April 21, 1509 |
| Buried at: | Westminster |
| Succeeded by: | His son Henry VIII |

Margaret, was a descendant of Edward III through John of Gaunt. The death of the imprisoned Henry VI made Henry Tudor head of the house of Lancaster. At this point, however, the Yorkist Edward IV had established himself securely on the throne, and Henry fled to Brittany.

The death of Edward IV and accession of Richard III, left Henry the natural leader of the party opposing Richard. Henry bided his time in France until 1485 when, aided by other English refugees, he landed in Wales. At the battle of Bosworth Field he defeated the royal armies of Richard, who was killed. Henry advanced to London, was crowned, and in 1486 married Edward IV's daughter and sister of the two "Princes in the Tower", Elizabeth of York. He thus united the houses of York and Lancaster, founding the Tudor royal dynasty.

Although Henry's accession marked the end of the Wars of the Roses, there were further uprisings in attempts to claim the throne, the first by a young Lambert Simnel, who claimed to be Richard one of the "Princes in the Tower".

Another pretender, Perkin Warbeck, sought support from the Scottish king, James IV. However, a truce between England and Scotland was followed by the marriage of Henry's daughter Margaret Tudor to James. This marriage led ultimately to the union of the monarchies of England and Scotland.

Henry married his eldest son Arthur to Catherine of Aragón, daughter of Ferdinand II of Aragón and Isabella of Castile Arthur died in 1502 and Henry arranged a dispensation from the Pope so that his younger son, Henry could marry Catherine.

Henry VII died of tuberculosis.

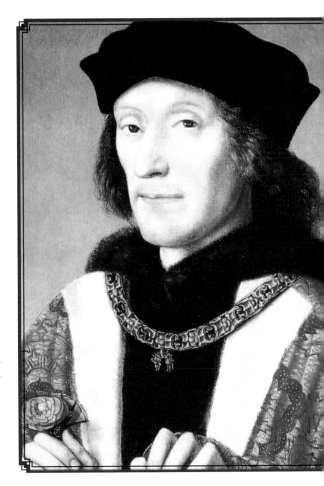

# King Henry VIII

RIGHT King Henry VIII
by Hans Holbein
the younger

Henry VIII became king at the age of about eighteen, when he succeeded his father Henry VII. He married Catherine of Aragon, the widow of his elder brother Arthur which helped form a diplomatic alliance with Spain against France.

| | |
|---|---|
| Born: | June 28, 1491 at Greenwich Palace |
| Parents: | Henry VII and Elizabeth of York |
| House of: | Tudor |
| Became King: | April 21, 1509 |
| Married: | (1) Catherine of Aragon, (2) Anne Boleyn, (3) Jane Seymour, (4) Anne of Cleves, (5) Catherine Howard, (6) Catherine Parr |
| Children: | 3 legitimate, and at least 1 illegitimate child |
| Died: | January 28, 1547 |
| Buried at: | Windsor |
| Succeeded by: | His son Edward VI |

Under the guidance of his Lord Chancellor, Cardinal Wolsey, Henry set out to make England stronger. Catherine bore him a daughter, Mary, but no son..

Now Henry was obsessed with his desire to divorce Catherine because she was too old to give him another heir and he was determined to marry Anne Boleyn. At first there seemed a possibility that the divorce might be granted. The papal legate journeyed to England to hear the case, but Catherine appealed direct to the pope and the court was adjourned. Her nephew, Charles V controlled Rome.

Henry blamed Wolsey for failing to persuade the Pope to grant a divorce, and he stripped Wolsey of all his wealth, banished from court and then accused him of treason. Henry proceeded to act through Parliament, and had the entire body of the clergy in England declared guilty of treason in 1531. The clergy were suitably browbeaten and agreed to renounce papal supremacy and recognize Henry as supreme head of the church in England. The English ecclesiastical courts then pronounced his marriage to Catherine null and void and so he married Anne Boleyn.

Henry through Thomas Cromwell continued his attack on the church with the repression of the monasteries; their lands were confiscated and granted to his supporters. However, although he laid the ground for the English Reformation by the separation from Rome, he had little sympathy with Protestant dogmas.

Henry's second wife, Anne Boleyn bore him another daughter, Elizabeth, but was beheaded in 1536, for adultery. Quite soon after the death of Anne, Henry married Jane Seymour, who bore him his son, Edward. Jane died a few days after the birth.

Thomas Cromwell then arranged for Henry to marry Anne of Cleves, a

German princess. Unfortunately Henry was not happy when he saw her. Henry called Anne "the Flanders Mare" and reportedly their marriage was never consummated. A divorce was agreed. and Cromwell beheaded.

His fifth wife, a cousin of Anne Boleyn, was Catherine Howard. Henry discovered that she had probably been unfaithful and so she was beheaded as well. The following year he married his sixth wife,

Catherine Parr, who proved to be a good companion in Henry's last years and a good stepmother to the three children. She outlived Henry.

Henry ended his reign with the reputation of being a tyrant. However, the power of the crown had been considerably strengthened by Henry's religious policy, and the monastic confiscations gave impetus to the rise of a new nobility which was to become influential in succeeding reigns.

LEFT 18 yr old Henry after his coronation

BELOW The meeting of Francis I and Henry VIII at the Field of the Cloth of Gold in 1520

# King Edward VI

Due to his young age, Edward's reign was initially governed by The Lord Protector, Edward Seymour (Duke of Somerset), and then to the Earl of Warwick, later created Duke of Northumberland.

| | |
|---|---|
| Born: | October 12, 1537 at Hampton Court |
| Parents: | Henry VIII and Jane Seymour |
| House of: | Tudor |
| Became King: | January 28, 1547 |
| Married: | Unmarried |
| Children: | None |
| Died: | July 6, 1553 |
| Buried at: | Westminster |
| Succeeded by: | His half sister Mary |

Edward became a staunch Protestant, and during his reign the Reformation progressed. He died of tuberculosis, and his will, probably prepared by the Duke of Northumberland, set aside that of his father so as to exclude his half-sisters, Mary and Elizabeth, from the succession. He nominated Lady Jane Grey, a granddaughter of Henry VII, who had recently married Northumberland's son Lord Guildford Dudley and wanted to maintain a Protestant succession.

Meanwhile, Henry's daughter Mary, Edward's half sister, was also proclaimed queen. The situation was resolved when 9 days later Mary and her supporters rode into London and she was accepted as queen and crowned.

# 42

# Queen Mary I

RIGHT "Bloody Mary" England's first reigning queen was a woman of strong convictions

FAR RIGHT The Tudor Princess – Mary in 1544

When Edward VI died, Mary secured the crown without difficulty in spite of a conspiracy to substitute Lady Jane Grey.

Mary is remembered for her restoration of Roman Catholicism after the short-lived Protestant reign of her half-brother, Edward.

| | |
|---|---|
| Born: | February 8, 1516 at Greenwich Palace |
| Parents: | Henry VIII and Catherine of Aragon |
| House of: | Tudor |
| Became Queen: | July 19, 1553 |
| Married: | Philip II of Spain |
| Children: | None |
| Died: | November 17, 1558 |
| Buried at: | Westminster |
| Succeeded by: | Her half sister Elizabeth |

In 1554 Mary married Philip II of Spain – mainly to produce an heir so that her Protestant sister, Elizabeth, would not succeed to the throne. It is said that Philip had no amorous feelings towards Mary and sought the marriage for its political and strategic gains only.

Mary was determined to eradicate Protestantism and during her five-year reign, she had over 280 religious dissenters burned at the stake. The number of executions earned her the name 'Bloody Mary'.

In January 1556, Mary's father-in-law

abdicated and Philip became King of Spain, with Mary as his consort. Philip was declared king in Brussels, but Mary stayed in England.

Mary never bore an heir, despite a couple of "phantom" pregnancies and had to accept that her half-sister, Elizabeth, was her lawful successor.

# 43

# Queen Elizabeth I

Her mother, Anne Boleyn, was executed when Elizabeth was just two and half years old. She was well educated in several languages. During Mary I's reign, Elizabeth's Protestant sympathies brought her under suspicion, and she lived in seclusion at Hatfield, Hertfordshire, until on Mary's death she became queen at the age of 25. Sometimes referred to or nicknamed "The Virgin Queen", "Gloriana" or "Good Queen Bess", Elizabeth was the fifth and last Tudor monarch.

Elizabeth depended on a few trusted advisers, the chief one being William Cecil, Baron Burghley. an English statesman, and one of her first moves as queen was to establish an English Protestant church, which later evolved into today's Church of England. Elizabeth had a favourite, Robert Dudley, Earl of Leicester, who was a childhood friend. The Queen's friendship with Dudley lasted for over thirty years, until his death. It was expected that Elizabeth would marry and then produce an heir so as to continue the Tudor dynasty. But she never did – and there were many

| | |
|---|---|
| Born: | September 7, 1533 at Greenwich Palace |
| Parents: | Henry VIII and Anne Boleyn |
| House of: | Tudor |
| Became Queen: | November 17, 1558 |
| Married: | Unmarried |
| Children: | None |
| Died: | March 24, 1603 |
| Buried at: | Westminster |
| Succeeded by: | Her 3rd cousin James of Scotland |

unsuccessful attempts by Parliament to persuade her. She did, however, have various courtships and used these as a political weapon. Some of these were maintained as friendships, notably Sir Walter Raleigh and Robert Devereux, Earl of Essex.

A threat to Elizabeth's reign came in the form of her cousin, Mary, Queen of Scots – who was a Catholic. Elizabeth imprisoned Mary and kept her under constant surveillance for 19 years. There were many conspiracies and plots to put Mary on the English throne, but Elizabeth showed caution and was reluctant to act against her. However, in 1586 a conspiracy was uncovered called the Babington plot which implicated Mary directly. Mary was tried for treason and executed in 1587. In 1588 Philip II of Spain launched the Spanish Armada, to try and overthrow Elizabeth. With a combination of bad weather, misfortune, and an attack of English fire ships under the command of Sir Francis Drake, the Armada was defeated.

Elizabeth's health was fine until the autumn of 1602, when she fell into severe depression after the deaths of some of her close friends In March, Elizabeth fell sick and remained in a "settled and unremovable melancholy." She died on 24 March 1603 aged nearly 70, after 45 years of being queen.

The Elizabethan age was often called "the golden age", and arts and literature flourished. During this period William Shakespeare and Christopher Marlowe created poetry and drama while composers such as William Byrd and Thomas Tallis worked in Elizabeth's court.

BELOW Elizabeth I in her coronation robes, patterned with Tudor roses and trimmed with ermine

# King James I

James's parent's marriage was short and his father was murdered 8 months after James was born. His mother married again, but was forced to renounce the throne of Scotland in

| Born: | June 19, 1566 at Edinburgh Castle, Scotland |
|---|---|
| Parents: | Mary, Queen of Scots and Henry Stewart, Lord Darnley |
| House of: | Stuart |
| Became King: | March 24, 1603 |
| Married: | Anne, Daughter of Frederick II of Denmark and Norway |
| Children: | 3 sons and 5 daughters |
| Died: | March 27, 1625 |
| Buried at: | Westminster |
| Succeeded by: | His son Charles |

favour of her infant son. James became King James VI of Scotland aged 13 months in July 1567, and was crowned at Stirling.

James was seen as the most likely heir to the English throne through his great-grandmother Margaret Tudor, who was Henry VIII's oldest sister. From 1601, in the last years of Elizabeth I's life, some English politicians, mainly Sir Robert Cecil, had a secret correspondence with James to prepare for a smooth succession. In March 1603, with the Queen clearly dying, Cecil sent James a draft proclamation of his accession to the English throne.

James was the first of the Stuart Kings to combine the crowns of England and Scotland. He proclaimed himself King of

Great Britain and a new Anglo-Scottish flag was introduced for shipping, which combined the cross of St. George and St. Andrew – it was called the "Great Union" flag – which later became the "Union Jack". He commissioned the King James Authorized Version of the Bible, published in 1611, which remains one of the most important English translations of the Bible.

During his reign, a plot aimed to depose the Protestant James was led by Guy Fawkes' whose attempt to blow up Parliament in 1605 produced an anti-Catholic reaction, which gave James a temporary popularity, which didn't last long.

During his reign the East India Company expanded trade bringing spices from the East, and Jamestown was founded in Virginia.

James and Anne had 8 children only three of whom survived infancy. Their eldest son Henry died aged 18 of typhoid, and their 2nd son Charles became King Charles I. The marriage of their daughter Elizabeth to Frederic V, Elector Palatine and King of Bohemia, was to result in the eventual Hanoverian succession to the British throne.

# 45

# King Charles I

RIGHT Portrait of
Charles I in 1628

Born in Scotland, Charles was a weak and sickly infant. It is thought he suffered from rickets, but also his speech development was slow, and he had a stammer for the rest of his life.

| | |
|---|---|
| Born: | November 19, 1600 |
| | at Dunfermline Palace, Scotland |
| Parents: | James I (VI of Scots) and |
| | Anne of Denmark |
| House of: | Stuart |
| Became King: | March 27, 1625 |
| Married: | Henrietta Maria, |
| | Daughter of Henri IV |
| Children: | 4 sons and 5 daughters |
| Died: | January 30, 1649 |
| Buried at: | Windsor |
| Succeeded by: | His son Charles II |

In 1603 due to his fragile health, Charles's parents and older siblings left him in Scotland under the care of one his father's friends, who was appointed his guardian.

When Charles was three and a half he was able to walk the length of the great hall at Dunfermline Palace without assistance, so it was decided that he was strong enough to make the journey to England to be reunited with his family.

Charles became heir apparent to the English, Irish and Scottish thrones on the death of his elder brother in 1612.

His father wanted Charles to marry the Spanish princess, Maria Anna, but Parliament was hostile to Spain and so in

LEFT A nineteenth century painting depicting Charles (centre in blue sash) before the battle of Edgehill, 1642

1625 he married Henrietta Maria, daughter of Henry IV of France. Their children included Charles and James (who became Charles II and James II), and Mary who married William II of Orange and was the mother of William III.

As soon as Charles became king there was friction with Parliament. Charles believed in his divine right as king and struggled to control Parliament. He actually dissolved Parliament three times between 1625 and 1629. In 1629 he resolved to rule alone which forced him to raise funds without the consent of Parliament, which made him even more unpopular. Charles was a very religious man and he preferred church services to be grand and full of ritual and colour. This led to a clash with many in England who preferred plain and simple services. In 1637, Charles tried to impose a new prayer book on the Scots. The Scots wanted simple prayer services, but the new prayer book required more splendour.

This clash led to the Scots invading England and occupying Durham and Newcastle.

Charles was forced to call parliament to obtain funds to fight the Scots, but demands were placed on Charles which he believed challenged the divine right of kings to govern as they saw fit. Charles attempted to have five key members of Parliament arrested but they fled to London, and in August 1642, Charles raised the royal standard at Nottingham calling on all loyal subjects to support him. Civil war had begun.

The Royalists were defeated by a combination of parliament's alliance with the Scots and the formation of the New Model Army. Charles surrendered to the Scots, who handed him over to parliament. Charles was put him on trial for treason. He was found guilty and executed on 30 January 1649 outside the Banqueting House on Whitehall, London.

There followed a period known as the English Commonwealth ruled by a principal commander of the New Model Army, Oliver Cromwell, through parliament.

# 46

# King Charles II

In 1645, Charles Stuart, the heir to the Crown, had to flee from England and for the next 5 years was in exile in France.

An attempt was made to invade England but was ended on 3 September 1651 by Cromwell's victory at the Battle of Worcester. Legend says that Charles hid in an oak tree to escape capture. The death

of Oliver Cromwell and the subsequent collapse of the English Commonwealth opened up negotiations in 1659 by George Monk for the restoration of the monarchy. The newly elected Convention Parliament was mainly pro-royalist and approved the restoration of Charles as King.

Charles was proclaimed King on 8 May 1660. He landed at Dover on 26 May, and entered London three days later on his 30th birthday. Crowds lined the streets cheering and throwing flowers and celebrating the restoration of the monarchy. In May 1662 Charles married the Portuguese Princess Catherine of Braganza. Despite four pregnancies she produced no children. Charles had many mistresses while King of Great Britain. Probably the most famous was Nell Gwynn. Others included Lucy Walter and the Duchess of Portsmouth. It is said he had 17 illegitimate children.

| | |
|---|---|
| Born: | May 29, 1630 at St. James Palace |
| Parents: | Charles I and Henrietta Maria |
| House of: | Stuart |
| Became King: | May 29, 1660 |
| Married: | Catherine of Braganza |
| Children: | 3, and about 17 illegitimate children |
| Died: | February 6, 1685 |
| Buried at: | Westminster |
| Succeeded by: | His brother James II |

LEFT A King in exile

The Restoration brought social changes including the re-opening of theatres and study of sciences that had been banned by the Puritans. The Royal Society for the study of Science was established and the Royal Observatory at Greenwich. Charles was known as "The Merry Monarch", and was a lover of sports and games. He loved entertainment and had an easy-going manner.

In 1664 an English fleet seized the Dutch settlement at New Amsterdam on the Hudson river in North America and renamed it New York. The Dutch General, Peter Stuyvesant did not resist. However the next year the Dutch declared war on England. In 1665 following a heat wave in June a bubonic plague hit the country with 70,000 dying in London alone. The following year the Great Fire of London hit London, destroying St Paul's and 13,000 homes and making 100,000 homeless.

In 1670 Charles signed the Secret Treaty of Dover, promising King Louis XIV of France he would declare himself a Catholic, re-establish Catholicism in England, and support the French king's projected war against the Dutch. Louis was to finance Charles and if needed supply him with troops. Another Dutch War followed in 1672. In 1673, Parliament forced Charles to accept a Test Act excluding all Catholics from office, and in 1674 to end the Dutch war. In 1678 Titus Oates's announcement of a 'Popish plot' released a general panic, which was exploited to exclude Charles's brother James, Duke of York, from the succession as he was openly Catholic and instead he hoped to substitute Charles's illegitimate son the Duke of Monmouth. Charles dissolved Parliament in 1679 declaring there would be no talk of change of succession. He now ruled as monarch without a parliament, financed by Louis XIV. When a revolt was uncovered, the leaders were executed, and Monmouth fled to the Netherlands to William of Orange. Charles died in 1685, becoming a Roman Catholic on his deathbed.

# King James II

James's parent's marriage was short and his father was murdered 8 months after James was born. His mother married again, but was forced to renounce the throne of Scotland in favour of her infant son. James became King James VI of Scotland aged 13 months in July 1567, and was crowned at Stirling.

| | |
|---|---|
| Born: | October 14, 1633 at St. James Palace |
| Parents: | Charles I and Henrietta Maria |
| House of: | Stuart |
| Became King: | February 6, 1685 |
| Married: | (1) Anne Hyde, (2) Mary, Daughter of Duke of Modena |
| Children: | 8 by his first wife Anne and 5 by his 2nd wife Mary |
| Died: | September 6, 1701 |
| Buried at: | Chateau de Saint Germain-en-Laye, Near Paris |
| Succeeded by: | His daughter Mary and son-in-law William of Orange |

James was created Duke of York, and was in Oxford during the Civil War. After the defeat of the Royalists he escaped with his mother and brother to exile in France. He served in the French army and then in the Spanish Army. After the death of Cromwell and the restoration of the monarchy he returned to England where his brother had been crowned king.

James was created Lord High Admiral and warden of the Cinque Ports, and commanded the Royal Navy during the 2nd and 3rd Anglo-Dutch wars.

He created controversy when in 1660 he married Anne Hyde a commoner and daughter of Charles's chief minister Edward Hyde. They had 7 children, although only two survived infancy - Mary (later Queen Mary II) and Anne (later Queen Anne). His daughters were raised as Protestants but, James converted to Catholicism. Following Anne's death in 1671, he married Mary of Modena a 15 year old Italian Catholic princess.

James became King James II on the death of his brother in 1685 and almost immediately had to deal with a Protestant revolt and challenge in the form of the Duke of Monmouth (Charles's illegitimate son). Monmouth's army was defeated by John Churchill (6th great grandfather of Winston Churchill) in July 1685 at the Battle of Sedgemoor in Somerset. Monmouth was executed.

James promoted his Catholic supporters into high posts in the army which provoked widespread alarm in Parliament. In 1688 his Catholic heir James (James Edward Stuart) was born which prompted a group of nobles to invite Prince William of Orange (who had married James' daughter Mary) from the Netherlands to England to restore Protestantism and democracy.

Prince William of Orange landed at Torbay on 5 November 1688 and with an army of 14,000 troops gathered West Country support as they advanced on London in what became known as 'The Glorious Revolution'. Many from James's army, including Churchill and James's daughter Anne, defected to support William.

James fled to France throwing the Great Seal of the Realm into the River Thames. His daughter Mary was declared Queen.

James and his wife and son lived in exile in France as guests of Louis XIV. James landed in Ireland in 1689 with French troops in an attempt to regain the throne and advanced on Londonderry, but was defeated by William at the Battle of the Boyne in 1690.

He lived the rest of his life in exile. His son James Edward Stuart (The Old Pretender) and grandson Charles (Bonnie Prince Charlie) made unsuccessful attempts to restore the Jacobite throne.

ABOVE Portrait of King James II, 1660s

# King William III

William was born in The Hague in the Netherlands and was subsequently nicknamed "Dutch Billy". In 1677 he married his cousin Mary. The marriage was intended to restore relations between England and The Netherlands following the Anglo-Dutch wars. William never very popular with his people, his character was very different from the flamboyant Charles II, as he had an unattractive manner, was short and suffered from severe asthma. He was also 12 years older and several inches shorter than his English wife Mary.

England needed a Protestant monarch and In 1688 Mary and William were invited by the parliamentary opposition to Mary's father James II to take the crown on England and were assured of English support. After James II fled to France, William and his wife were crowned King William III and Queen Mary II. Parliament then passed the Bill of Rights which prevented Catholics for

| | |
|---|---|
| Born: | November 14, 1650 at The Hague, Netherlands |
| Parents: | William II of Orange and Mary Stuart |
| House of: | Orange |
| Became King: | February 13, 1689 |
| Married: | William married Mary, daughter of James II |
| Died: | March 8, 1702 |
| Buried at: | Westminster |
| Succeeded by: | Mary's sister Anne |

succeeding to the throne ensuring that Mary's sister Anne would become the next queen.

There were two Jacobite attempts to regain the throne. In Scotland government troops were defeated at Killiekrankie by Scottish Jacobites but won shortly afterwards at Dunkeld, and then the deposed James II landed in Ireland with French troops and laid siege to Londonderrry. William landed in Ireland with a vast army and inflicted a decisive defeat on James's army at the Battle of the Boyne in July 1690. James fled back to France and William returned to England

Mary died of smallpox in 1694, she was just 32. William was devastated by the death of his wife and he now ruled alone. William formed an alliance between England, Holland and Austria to prevent the union of the French and Spanish crowns. This became known as the 'War of Spanish Succession'. In 1701 following death of Prince William, the only surviving son of Mary's sister Anne, the Act of Settlement was passed ensuring succession of Protestant heirs of Sophie of Hanover instead of the Catholic heirs of James.

In 1702 William fell from his horse and broke his collarbone, after the animal stumbled over a molehill. William developed a fever and died. Happy Jacobites toasted 'the little gentleman in the black velvet waistcoat" referring to the mole.'

BELOW Portrait of King William III

# Queen Anne

After her father, James converted to Catholicism, Anne and her elder sister Mary received a Protestant upbringing. In 1683 Anne married Prince George of Denmark. She had between 16 and 18 pregnancies but only one child survived - William, Duke of Gloucester who died aged 11 of smallpox

| Full Name: | Anne Stuart |
|---|---|
| Born: | February 6, 1665 at St. James Palace, London |
| Parents: | James II and Anne Hyde |
| House of: | Stuart |
| Became Queen: | March 8, 1702 |
| Married: | George, son of Frederick III of Denmark |
| Children: | 1 that survived to infancy |
| Died: | August 1, 1714 |
| Buried at: | Westminster |
| Succeeded by: | Her 3rd cousin George of Hanover |

Her sister Mary married William of Orange but Anne was forbidden by her father to visit her in the Netherlands. When William landed in England in 1688 to take the throne, Anne supported her sister and brother-in-law against her father James.

When she was crowned in April 1702 Anne was 37 years old and after her many pregnancies had poor health and no longer her youthful figure. She suffered from rheumatism and gout and could only walk a short distance with a stick. Anne's close friend, Sarah Churchill's husband the Duke of Marlborough commanded the English Army in the War of Spanish Succession, and won a series of victories over the French The influence of the Churchill's however began to decline and after a violent quarrel, Sarah Churchill was dismissed from court. A new favourite, Abigail Masham, who was a relation of Sarah's, remained close to the queen.

On her death in 1714 Anne's body had swollen so large that she was buried in an almost square coffin.

On the question of succession, Anne's family loyalty had convinced her that this should fall to her father's son by his second wife, James Edward Stuart, known as the Old Pretender. However, the Act of Settlement in 1701 ensured Protestant succession to the throne, and Anne was succeeded by George I, great-grandson of James I.

# King George I

Prince George Louis, Elector of Brunswick-Luneburg was declared King George I less than 9 hours after Queen Anne died. He was aged 54.

| | |
|---|---|
| Full Name: | George Louis |
| Born: | May 28, 1660 at Osnabruck, Hanover |
| Parents: | Ernst August, Duke of Brunswick and Sophia Stuart |
| House of: | Hanover |
| Became King: | August 1, 1714 |
| Married: | Sophia Dorothea of Celle |
| Children: | 1 son, 1 daughter, 3 illegitimate children |
| Died: | June 11, 1727 |
| Buried at: | Leineschlosskirche, Hanover |
| Succeeded by: | His son George II |

George's claim to the throne of England was mainly as a Protestant with a distant blood relationship to the ruling line. His mother, Sophia was a granddaughter of James I of England.

Although George had several mistresses, he imprisoned his wife, Sophia in Castle Ahlden in Germany for having a love affair. George also banned Sophia from seeing her son, the Prince of Wales, which caused a "falling out" between father and son.

George only spoke a few words of English, and never learned more. He also was not interested in British customs and certainly did not gain any affection by his British subjects.

The king grew frustrated in his attempts

to control Parliament and more and more dependent upon his advisers as scandal surrounded him; his supporters turned against him, demanding freedom of action as the price of reconciliation. George rarely attended meetings with his ministers, and particularly Robert Walpole, who became powerful and in effect was Britain's first Prime Minister.

Supporters of James Edward Stuart (James II's son) rebelled in Scotland in 1715 led by Lord Mar, and in 1719 supported by Spanish troops intending to place James 'The Old Pretender' on the throne found little support and were quickly defeated.

The 'South Sea Bubble' in which shares in companies were purchased in rash financial speculation before a stock market crash in 1720 left many investors ruined. George and the royal family were left looking corrupt and implicated in the scandal. However, the royal court survived because of Robert Walpole's management of the debts and paying compensation using Government money helped return financial stability.

George spent more and more time in Hanover where he died of a stroke in 1727.

# 51

# King George II

George, Prince of Wales became the second ruler of the house of Hanover just four days after his father's death.

| | |
|---|---|
| Full Name: | George Augustus |
| Born: | October 30, 1683 |
| | at Herrenhausen, Hanover |
| Parents: | George I and Sophia Dorothea |
| House of: | Hanover |
| Became King: | June 11, 1727 |
| Married: | Caroline, daughter of Margrave |
| | of Brandenburg |
| Children: | 4 sons and 5 daughters |
| Died: | October 25, 1760 |
| Buried at: | Westminster |
| Succeeded by: | His grandson George III |

He was married to Caroline of Brandenburg-Ansbach - and they had 9 children. Caroline was a popular consort and influenced George to keep her close friend Sir Robert Walpole as chief government minister.

Even though he was devoted to his Queen, George had two mistresses and openly kept them in St. James's Palace.

The death of Holy Roman Emperor Charles VI in 1740 led to the European War of Austrian Succession in which the British and Dutch supported Marie Theresa's claim to the Austrian throne against the Prussians and French. George II personally led his troops at the Battle of Dettingen in 1743, becoming the last British monarch to lead his troops into battle. The Jacobite Rebellion of 1745, in which Charles Edward Stuart ('Bonnie Prince Charlie') landed in Scotland and marched with a Highland army into England, was defeated at Culloden in 1746 and Scottish opposition brutally suppressed by George's second son Prince William, Duke of Cumberland.

Like his father, George quarreled with his eldest son Frederick, Prince of Wales, over his marriage but Frederick died suddenly in 1751.

The final years of his reign saw George retiring from active politics; however it was a period in which British dominance overseas grew. William Pitt became Prime Minister during the Seven years war against France which spread to India and North America. Robert Clive secured the Indian continent for Britain at the Battle of Plassey, and General Wolfe captured Quebec in Canada.

George II died in 1760 of a heart attack whilst seated on the toilet.

# 52

# King George III

George became heir to the throne when his father died in 1751, succeeding his grandfather George II in 1760. He was the first Hanoverian monarch to be born in England and to speak English as his first language. In 1761, George married Charlotte of Mecklenburg-Strelitz and they enjoyed a happy marriage, and they had 16 children.

George was shy and stubborn but well educated in science and arts. In 1762 he bought Buckingham House in London which later became Buckingham Palace.

George had high moral standards, and was concerned that the royal family should set a good example to their subjects – he introduced the Royal Marriage Act in 1772 which made it illegal for members of the Royal Family to marry without the consent of the Sovereign.

George ended the Seven Years' War.

| | |
|---|---|
| Full Name: | George William Frederick |
| Born: | June 4, 1738 |
| Parents: | Frederick Prince of Wales and Augusta of Saxe-Gotha |
| House of: | Hanover |
| Became King: | October 25, 1760 |
| Married: | Charlotte, daughter of Duke of Mecklenburg-Strelitz |
| Children: | 10 sons, and 6 daughters |
| Died: | January 29, 1820 |
| Buried at: | Windsor |
| Succeeded by: | His son George IV |

The American War of Independence began in April. On 4 July 1776 the Continental Congress declared independence. Fighting continued until 1781 when the British were defeated by Americans and French at Yorktown. Britain agreed to recognise American independence, but King George took the loss badly and considered abdication.

In 1788 he suffered his first attack of insanity which also affected his eyesight. He also started behaving violently and confused and was confined in a straightjacket in 1810 – his son George was made Prince Regent.

George III's illness (now believed to be the result of the inherited disease porphyria) was to plague him for the rest of his life and he became a pathetic figure, completely blind and increasingly deaf with long straggling white hair and beard.

George III died at Windsor Castle on 29 January 1820, after a reign of almost 60 years - the third longest in British history.

LEFT King George III was admired for his upright character

This caused outrage for the concessions it gave to the French including the rights of French colonists in North America to remain in Quebec and New Orleans. Lord North became Prime Minister determined to make the colonies pay for their own security. The Stamp Act of 1765 levied a tax on every official document in the British colonies. These were mostly repealed in the face of American opposition, except the tax on tea. In 1773 colonists threw chests of tea overboard in Boston harbour in a protest know as the 'Boston Tea Party'.

# King George IV

George IV, as Prince of Wales, was Regent from 1810 to 1820 during his father's period of insanity. George IV was extravagant with money and known for his excesses in food, drink, women and gambling. In 1785, George secretly and illegally married a Roman Catholic, Maria Fitzherbert. This was in contravention of the Act of Settlement and the Royal Marriage Act, put in place by his father.

George commissioned John Nash to build the Royal Pavilion in Brighton and remodel Buckingham Palace, and Sir Jeffry Wyattville to rebuild Windsor Castle. He was instrumental in the foundation of the National Gallery and King's College London.

George was forced to deny his marriage with Mrs Fitzherbert and in return for paying off his mounting debts officially marry Caroline of Brunswick whom

| | |
|---|---|
| Full Name: | George Augustus Frederick |
| Born: | August 12, 1762 |
| Parents: | George III and Charlotte of Mecklenburg-Strelitz |
| House of: | Hanover |
| Became King: | January 29, 1820 |
| Married: | Caroline, daughter of Duke of Brunswick |
| Children: | 1 daughter, and at least 2 illegitimate children |
| Died: | June 26, 1830 |
| Buried at: | Windsor |
| Succeeded by: | His brother William IV |

he hated. They had only one child, Princess Charlotte, who died at the age of 21 during childbirth. George refused to recognise Caroline as Queen and tried several times to annul his marriage to her. She died in 1821 claiming on her death bed that she had been poisoned.

King George IV paid a state visit to Scotland in 1822, the first monarch to do so since Charles II, and encouraged by Sir Walter Scott wore full Highland regalia leading to a revival of Scottish tartan dress that had been banned after the Jacobite Rebellions.

His heavy drinking, indulgent lifestyle and taste for huge amounts of food made him obese, and he became an unpopular figure of ridicule when he appeared in public.

He suffered from gout and towards the end of his life became mentally unstable. He died of a heart attack at Windsor Castle in 1830.

# King William IV

William was the third son of George III and not expected to become king. He inherited the throne when he was 64. He was sent off to join the Royal Navy at 13 years old, and saw service at the Battle of St Vincent against the Spanish in 1780 and in New York during the American War of Independence. He was stationed in the West Indies under Horatio Nelson, and left active service in 1790 as a Rear Admiral. He was made Duke of Clarence. He was later nicknamed "The Sailor King".

William lived with his mistress, the actress Dorothy Jordan for 20 years. They had 10 children who took the surname Fitzclarence. But when he became heir to the throne he married Adelaide of Saxe-Meiningen in 1818. The marriage was happy but despite several miscarriages there were no children who survived infancy. His London residence

| | |
|---|---|
| Full Name: | William Henry |
| Born: | August 21, 1765 |
| Parents: | George III and Charlotte of Mecklenburg-Strelitz |
| House of: | Hanover |
| Became King: | June 26, 1830 |
| Married: | Adelaide, daughter of Duke of Saxe-Meinigen |
| Children: | 4 – with his queen - none of whom survived infancy and 10 illigitimate children |
| Died: | June 20, 1837 |
| Buried at: | Windsor |
| Succeeded by: | His niece Victoria |

Clarence House was designed for him by John Nash in 1825.

William was popular with his people, and he took his responsibilities seriously. His reign saw several reforms: the poor law was updated, child labour restricted, slavery abolished in nearly all the British Empire, and the British electoral system refashioned by the Reform Act 1832. William gained a new nickname "Reform Billy".

William died in 1837 aged 71 of heart failure. He had no legitimate children and was succeeded by his niece Victoria.

# Queen Victoria

Known as Victoria, she was the only child of Edward Duke of Kent and Victoria Saxe-Coburg. Her father died when she was 1 year old and her domineering mother raised under close supervision. She had a sheltered upbringing, and came to the throne shortly after her 18th birthday in 1837 on the death of her uncle William IV. She was at the time unmarried and not crowned until June 28, 1838. In February 1840 she married her first cousin, Prince Albert of Saxe-Coburg and Gotha.

On her accession, Victoria adopted the Whig prime minister Lord Melbourne as her political adviser. In 1840, his influence was replaced by that of Prince Albert. The German prince never really won the favour of the British public, and only after 17 years was he given official recognition, with the title of 'prince consort'. Britain was evolving into a constitutional monarchy in which the monarch had

| | |
|---|---|
| Full Name: | Alexandrina Victoria |
| Born: | May 24, 1819 |
| Parents: | Edward, Duke of Kent (son of George III) and Victoria of Saxe-Coburg-Saalfeld |
| House of: | Hanover |
| Became Queen: | June 20, 1837 |
| Married: | Albert, son of Duke of Saxe-Coburg-Gotha |
| Children: | 4 sons, and 5 daughters |
| Died: | January 22, 1901 |
| Buried at: | Frogmore |
| Succeeded by: | Her son Edward VII |

few powers and was expected to remain above party politics, although Victoria did sometimes express her views very forcefully in private. The British Empire was at the height of its power and she ruled over 450 million people. The Victorian era was a time of immense industrial, political, trade, scientific and military progress for Great Britain.

Victoria and Albert had 9 children and 42 grandchildren who were married to royalty across Europe making her the 'grandmother of Europe'. Her daughter Victoria was mother of the German Emperor Kaiser Wilhelm II, and her grand-daughter Alexandria was the wife of Nicholas II Emperor and last Tzar of Russia.

Albert died from typhoid in 1861 - Victoria never fully recovered and she remained in mourning for the rest of her life. She withdrew almost completely from public life spending her time at Balmoral Castle in Scotland and Osborne house on the Isle of Wight where she spent time with her favourite Scottish servant John Brown. Victoria's self-imposed isolation from the public diminished the popularity of the monarchy.

Her golden jubilee in 1887 and diamond jubilee in 1897 regained her popular

support and matriarchal role as Queen of the Nation and Empire. She died at Osborne House on 22 January 1901 at the age of 81. Her reign lasted 63 years and 7 months which is the longest of any British monarch to date and the longest of any female monarch in history.

BELOW Victoria wearing her small diamond crown

# King Edward VII

Known to his family as 'Bertie', Edward came to the throne when he was 60. He was known as a playboy interested in horse racing, shooting, eating, drinking and other men's wives.

| Full Name: | Albert Edward |
|---|---|
| Born: | November 9, 1841 |
| Parents: | Queen Victoria and Albert of Saxe-Coburg-Gotha |
| House of: | Saxe-Coburg-Gotha |
| Became King: | January 22, 1901 |
| Married: | Alexandra, daughter of Christian of Denmark |
| Children: | 3 sons and 3 daughters |
| Died: | May 6, 1910 |
| Buried at: | Windsor |
| Succeeded by: | His son George V |

In 1863 he married Alexandra of Denmark and the marriage was a reasonably happy producing 6 children.

Edward had mistresses throughout his married life, most notably, the actress, Lillie Langtry; Lady Randolph Churchill (born Jennie Jerome, she was the mother of Winston Churchill); actress Sarah Bernhardt; noblewoman Lady Susan Vane-Tempest; singer Hortense Schneider; prostitute Giulia Beneni (known as "La Barucci"); wealthy Agnes Keyser; and Alice Keppel. One of Alice Keppel's great-granddaughters, Camilla Parker Bowles, became wife of Charles, Prince of Wales, one of Edward's great-great-grandsons. Edward never acknowledged any illegitimate children. Alexandra is believed to have been

America, but society was changing – socialism, women suffragettes, the Labour party and trade unions were becoming powerful and the founding of Britain's Welfare State. In an increasing democratic society Edward saw the importance of displaying the aura of pomp and circumstance of the monarchy, and seeing and being seen by the people.

Edward regularly smoked twenty cigarettes and twelve cigars a day. Towards the end of his life he increasingly suffered from bronchitis. He died at Buckingham Palace in 1910 and was succeeded by his second son George V.

**LEFT** Coronation portrait of King Edward VII

**BELOW** Edward VII relaxing at Balmoral Castle, photographed by his wife, Alexandra

aware of many of his affairs and to have accepted the situation.

When he became King Edward VII, Edward frequently made trips to Europe including France where he contributed to the Anglo-French 'Entente Cordiale' signed in 1904, to Russia and the Triple Entente between Britain, Russia and France which a few years later would play an important role in affairs on the outbreak of World War I. He supported reform of the army following the Boer War, and expansion of the Royal Navy including building the new Dreadnought battleships.

The Edwardian period was seen as golden age for the upper class in Europe and

# King George V

When George was 18 he went into the Royal Navy, but the death of his elder brother, Albert, meant he had to leave, as he was now heir to the throne. He married his elder brother's fiancée, Princess Mary of Teck in 1893.

George and Mary became Duke and Duchess of York and lived on the Sandringham Estate, in Norfolk. The marriage was a success and George, unlike his father, never took a mistress. They had 6 children Edward, Albert, Mary, Henry, George and John. The youngest Prince John suffered from epilepsy and died aged 13.

George became King George V on the death of his father Edward VII in 1910, and Mary became Queen consort. They toured India in 1911 as Emperor and Empress of India. She was a staunch supporter of her husband during difficult times that included not only the

| | |
|---|---|
| Full Name: | George Frederick Ernest Albert |
| Born: | June 3, 1865 |
| Parents: | Edward VII and Alexandra of Denmark |
| House of: | Windsor |
| Became King: | May 6, 1910 |
| Married: | Mary, the daughter of the Duke of Teck |
| Children: | 5 sons, and 1 daughter |
| Died: | January 20, 1936 |
| Buried at: | Windsor |
| Succeeded by: | His son Edward VIII |

war with Germany, but also the Russian revolution and murder of George's cousin Princess Alix who was the wife of Tsar Nicholas II. George V has been criticised for not rescuing the Russian Royal family, but at the time there was serious concern that it would incite a similar revolution in the UK.

Public respect for the king increased during World War One, when he made many visits to the front line, hospitals, factories and dockyards.

In 1917 with anti-German sentiment running high, he changed the family name from Saxe-Coburg-Gotha (popularly known as Brunswick or Hanover) to Windsor, and he relinquished all German titles and family connections.

George V enjoyed stamp collecting and although considered "dull" he became a much loved king by his Silver Jubilee in 1935. He started the tradition of the Royal Christmas broadcast which has continued ever since. His relationship deteriorated with this eldest son Edward (later Edward VIII) when he failed to settle down and had affairs with married women, but he was fond of his second

son Albert ("Bertie" later George VI) and his granddaughter Elizabeth (later Elizabeth II) whom he called 'Lilibet'. She called him 'Grandpa England'.

George V died of pleurisy in January 1936.

ABOVE King George V (right) and his physically similar cousin Emperor Nicholas II in German military uniforms in Berlin before the war.

# King Edward VIII

The reign of King Edward VIII lasted less than 11 months. Eldest son of King George V he was a popular Prince of Wales. He served in the Army during World War I but was not allowed to go to the front line. Known as David to his family, his relationship with his parents deteriorated as he became a celebrity playboy who failed to settle down and had several affairs with married women.

He became King Edward VIII in January 1936 on the death of his father George V. In November 1936 a constitutional crisis arose when Edward said he wished to marry divorcee, Mrs Wallis Simpson. On 11 December Edward abdicated and the couple left for France, where they were married in 1937.

Edward was succeeded by his brother Albert as George VI.

Edward and Wallis became The Duke

| Full Name: | Edward Albert Christian George Andrew Patrick David |
|---|---|
| Born: | June 23, 1894 |
| Parents: | George V and Mary of Teck |
| House of: | Windsor |
| Became King: | Jan 20, 1936 |
| Married: | Ms Wallis Simpson |
| Children: | None |
| Died: | May 28, 1972 |
| Buried at: | Frogmore |
| Succeeded by: | His brother George VI |

and Duchess of Windsor, but were ostracised by his family who felt he had let them down and not done his duty. His views of appeasement on the rise of fascism in Germany and Italy and meeting with Adolf Hitler in 1937 led him to be given the role during World War II of Governor of the Bahamas.

After the war Edward and Wallis became mild celebrities in Europe and America but lived mostly in Paris where he died in 1972. They had no children.

# King George VI

RIGHT Formal portrait of George VI

Second son of George V he was named Albert after his grandfather Prince Albert. As The Duke of York he had never expected or wished to succeed to the throne. He never lacked bravery or enterprise, and had a strong sense of Duty. He had fought as a young naval officer at the Battle of Jutland in World War I, and was the first member of the Royal Family to learn to fly. In 1923 he married Elizabeth Bowes-Lyon. They had two daughters Elizabeth, know as 'Lilibet' who later became Queen Elizabeth II, and Margaret Rose 'Princess Margaret'.

He became King George VI in December 1936 following the death of his father George V and the abdication of his brother. Fortified by the influence of his Queen, who swiftly acquired immense popularity in her own right, George VI coped with the aftermath of the abdication in a way that quickly restored confidence in the monarchy.

| | |
|---|---|
| Full Name: | Albert Frederick Arthur George |
| Born: | December 14, 1895 |
| Parents: | George V and Mary of Teck |
| House of: | Windsor |
| Became King: | Dec 11, 1936 |
| Married: | Elizabeth Bowes-Lyon |
| Children: | 2 daughters |
| Died: | February 6, 1952 |
| Buried at: | Windsor |
| Succeeded by: | His daughter Elizabeth II |

During the war George visited allied armies on several battle fronts and toured the home front. He created the George Cross for "acts of the greatest heroism". Initially sceptical of Winston Churchill, the King and his Prime Minister soon developed a close personal working relationship and they met regularly to discuss the progress of the War.

King George VI and Queen Elizabeth stayed at what they and their subjects saw as their posts all through the Blitz, and showed love and care for their people. They narrowly escaped death when bombs exploded beside Buckingham Palace.

George's hereditary title of Emperor of India ceased in 1947 when India and Pakistan became separate independent countries.

From 1948, his health deteriorated, and he died on 6 February 1952, a few months after undergoing an operation for lung cancer.

# Queen Elizabeth II

**Princess Elizabeth Alexandra Mary was born in London on 21 April 1926; she was educated privately, with her sister, Margaret.**

With the outbreak of World War II, Elizabeth and her sister, largely stayed out of London, spending much of their time at Windsor Castle. From there, she made one of her famous broadcasts. Over the radio, Elizabeth sought to reassure children who had been evacuated from their homes and families. The 14-year-old princess, showing her calm and firm personality, told them that "in the end, all will be well for God will care of us and

| | |
|---|---|
| Full Name: | Elizabeth Alexandra Mary |
| Born: | April 21, 1926 |
| Parents: | George VI and Elizabeth Bowes-Lyon |
| House of: | Windsor |
| Became Queen: | February 6, 1952 |
| Married: | Philip Mountbatten |
| Children: | 3 sons and 1 daughter (Charles, Anne, Andrew & Edward) |

give us victory and peace." Elizabeth soon started taking up other public duties. Appointed Colonel-in-Chief of the Grenadier Guards by her father, Elizabeth made her first public appearance inspecting the troops in 1942. She also began to accompany her parents on official visits within Great Britain.

In 1945, Elizabeth joined the Auxiliary Territorial Service to help in the war effort. She trained side-by-side with other British women to be an expert driver and mechanic. While her volunteer work only lasted a few months, it offered Elizabeth a glimpse into a different, non-royal world.

Elizabeth married Philip Mountbatten on 20 November 1947. Philip was the son of Prince Andrew of Greece and Denmark and he renounced his Greek nationality and became a British citizen (adopting the surname Mountbatten) before his engagement to Elizabeth. When they married, King George gave Philip the title Prince Philip, Duke of Edinburgh.

On 14 November 1948 Elizabeth gave birth to their first child, Charles, (now Prince Charles, the Prince of Wales the current heir to the throne) and on 15 August 1950 their daughter, Anne, was born.

# QUEEN ELIZABETH II

RIGHT Coronation
portrait of Queen
Elizabeth II and the
Duke of Edinburgh,
June 1953

BELOW Elizabeth in
Auxiliary Territorial
Service uniform,
April 1945

Elizabeth learned of the death of her father and therefore her elevation to the throne, on 6 February 1952 while on safari in Kenya with Prince Philip, and she was crowned on 2 June 1953. The coronation was a truly major television event, as it was the first televised coronation with around 120 million viewers in the UK and North America alone.

From the start of her reign, Elizabeth impressed all with the calm and dignity she displayed in taking on large responsibilities at the young age of 25. Her reign has seen major changes in her realms, such as devolution in the UK and patriation of the Canadian constitution. As hereditary head of State for Great Britain and Northern Ireland, and Head of the Commonwealth, she has symbolic and formal functions and duties but no direct powers.

The Queen and Prince Philip's first child Prince Charles was invested as Prince of Wales at Caernarvon Castle on 1 July 1969. He married

Lady Diana Spencer (Princess Diana) on 29 July 1981 – the wedding was called a "modern fairy tale" and took place in St. Paul's Cathedral. They had two sons, Prince William, born 21 June 1982 and Prince Henry (Harry), born 15 September 1984. Unfortunately, their marriage broke down amid widely-publicised bitterness, and a divorce followed.

These troubles, together with the divorces of their second child, Princess Anne, and their third, Andrew, the Duke of York, were seen by some to diminish the monarchy in public esteem, and on the night of 30 August 1997 Diana tragically died in a car crash in Paris. This caused a wave of hysteria, and the family had to suffer relentless intrusion by the world's press into their lives.

After the start of the 21st century, Elizabeth experienced two great losses. She said good-bye to both her sister Margaret and her mother in 2002. Margaret died that February after suffering a stroke. Only a few weeks later, Elizabeth's mother, known as the Queen Mother, died at Royal Lodge on March 30 at the age of 101.

Elizabeth has emerged as a devoted grandmother to Prince William and Prince Harry. Prince William has said that she offered invaluable support and guidance as he and Catherine Middleton planned their 2011 wedding.

Now in her late eighties, Elizabeth celebrated her Diamond Jubilee in 2013. The celebration marked her 60 years as queen. As part of the Jubilee festivities, a special service was held at Westminster Abbey on June 2nd, the 60th anniversary of her coronation. Elizabeth was surrounded by family at this historic event, including her husband Prince Philip, son Prince Charles and her grandsons Prince Harry and Prince William.

Elizabeth celebrated another happy event that July. Her grandson, Prince William, and his wife, Kate Middleton, welcomed their first child together, a son named George Alexander Louis—known officially as "His Royal Highness Prince George of Cambridge"—on July 22, 2013. Elizabeth visited her new great-grandson after William and Kate returned home to Kensington Palace from the hospital.

Elizabeth may even surpass Queen Victoria as Britain's longest ruling monarch who reigned for 63 years.

BELOW The Queen and Prince Philip with children and grandchildren

Design & Artwork: ALEX YOUNG

Published by: DEMAND MEDIA LIMITED

Publisher: JASON FENWICK

Written by: MARTINE PUGH